Trials of Today, Treasures for Tomorrow

Overcoming Adversities in Life

Janet Eckles

Contents

Part II: My Reflections

Part III: Study Group Guide

Dedication

I dedicate this book to the memory of our youngest son, Joe. His life was a gift to us for 19 years. He left us with his mark of strength and vitality. I live each moment focused on the glory of eternal life. My heart holds the certainty that we only said, 'Good night,' to Joe, and will be saying 'Good morning,' to him in heaven.

This reassurance that goes beyond hope gives me a new and refreshed look on life. It fills my moments with treasured memories of Joe. Along with the memories, I am comforted by the sustaining promise that Jesus has prepared a home for him. He prepared one for Joe, for me and for those who accept Him as their Savior.

At the time of this writing, Joe's "Mau Mau" (Terry), our son's step-grandmother also began her life in the glory of God. Her tender memories will be with us forever.

WWW.REMEMBERJOE.COM

A Note to the Reader

Understanding why tragedy happens is always difficult. Why do suffering and crisis occur? What I've found is that the "why" is not important, but the purpose they serve certainly is.

Almighty God, in His infinite wisdom allowed me to bring this book to reality. The contents are based on biblical principles. My hope is that they would speak to those who may be facing some unavoidable struggles, big or small.

Let me tell you a story—my story. As you read the personal details of my life, my goal is that you will find comfort, peace, and reassurance.

I divided the book in three parts. Part I relates my story. In Part II, I share with you my reflections on what I've survived. It answers the question, "What happens on the other side of adversity?" Part III can be used in a study group to bring out the biblical principles discussed in the book.

I don't believe in coincidence or chance. I believe in a powerful God who orchestrates every detail in each person's life. He might have had you in mind when He opened the door for me to share my journey with you. I invite you to walk with me through the episodes in my life. Together we'll see how tragedy was turned to triumph.

Acknowledgements

I am overwhelmed with gratitude to God and His mercy. He brought me to a point in my life where I can rejoice, in spite of the crisis that could have brought me to despair.

I thank my parents for their commitment to raising me in the knowledge of a faithful God. I admire my father for showing me his determination to overcome adversity. I am grateful to my mom, who is affectionately called "Ita." In her 4'11" and 100 lb frame, she has been a giant in my life. Her commitment to applying the Word of God each day and in every aspect of her life has been a beacon of light for me. She demonstrates the power of the written Word of God. She takes each step in her spiritual life guided by the verses in the Bible.

My husband has my admiration and gratitude for his constant support and unconditional love for me. His committed devotion and incomparable patience have been displayed in so many areas, including reviewing this book. His godly wisdom and endless qualities as a husband and father have been the jewels that adorn our 28 years of marriage.

I thank my three sons, Jason, Jeff, and also Joe, who now enjoys the glory of heaven. They filled my life with inexpressible joy. My deep desire has been, as I follow the Word of God, to honor and please Him in my role as their mom. I thank Jason and Jeff for providing encouragement to me during the writing of this book and Jason for drawing the beautiful illustrations.

I thank Dr. Ben Lerner because God used him to give me the encouragement that was instrumental as I moved forward with this writing. His insight and wise observations provided me with the framework I needed to relate my story. Ramona Richardson has my gratitude for patiently editing the final draft.

I'm also grateful to Sue and Ellen Key for their valuable input and logical suggestions regarding the contents of this book. Brad Basham has my gratitude for his diligent efforts in reviewing the text and study questions. I thank my dear friend, Nora Peters, for the generous way in which she applied her diligence and efficiency in reviewing the format of this writing. Thanks to my friends Sandy Mahone and Joy Adamek for their kind contribution.

Preface

"Those Bible preachers really get on my nerves," asserted my friend.

"I know what you mean. They sound so righteous as if they know it all!" I added with annoyance.

When it came to biblical teachings by religious preachers, skepticism, as well as a certain amount of critical judgment, marked my attitude. Although the unexpected adversity of an imminent blindness forced me to look beyond this narrow point of view, I had to first undergo a process to move past my *intolerant* mentality. I'd like to tell you how this came about.

My criticism toward the whole concept of preaching made clearing my mind about God and faith difficult. I had created a wall of arrogance. This critical attitude led me to doubt all those well-meaning preachers. They insisted that the Word of God was the solution to our problems. We would find the much-needed answers in the Scriptures, they affirmed. They claimed promises of salvation through Jesus. They proclaimed, "We must trust in God and His Word."

What did they know? Did they have any idea of what I was going through? Were they losing their sight like I was and soon facing complete blindness? Were they confronted with the overwhelming task of caring for three small sons without being able to even see their faces? How could they possibly identify with the turmoil I was going through?

Those were the questions that marked my skepticism and judgment of something I didn't know or want to know. Biblical concepts seemed irrelevant to my situation. I did not need an idea or an abstract concept. I needed a clear path for action that would restore my sight. If I wanted to look for answers, the countless self-help books would be a more logical place to find them. After all, the Bible, written so long ago, certainly couldn't hold any current or relevant guidance for me today. I saw the "Word of God" in the Bible as fleeting because it implied searching through that voluminous book just to find something to hang on to. Where do you begin? How do you know what is really meant for you?

Despite my skepticism, I still made a few feeble attempts to read Bible passages. They seemed ambiguous and difficult to grasp. As a result, I quickly dismissed the hope of finding any answers to the crisis I was facing. Nothing helped, and I became desperate. This is what led me to the very thing I had previously disregarded as unimportant.

But first I had to remove the shield of misguided and shamefully misinformed judgments. I took each step of this process with caution, as if I was scraping ice from a windshield. During some cold winter mornings when we lived in Missouri, my husband Gene had to scrape the ice off the windshield before driving the car. Once the ice was scraped away, inch by inch, with an ice scraper, the windshield was then clear enough to see the details of the road. As I began to search biblical teachings, I needed to use this same approach. I put into practice the process of "scraping" off the erroneous and misguided preconceptions I had of the Word of God. This gave me a clear view of what God was saying to me.

In the same way that an ice scraper was needed as a tool to clear the windshield, I also needed the tool of wisdom provided by the Holy Spirit. This was necessary in order to be able to understand God's Word. This way, the ambiguity eventually melted away providing a path for me to see my way through the worst moments of my life.

I humbly share my story—my process—with you. I do so, not with the authority of theological credentials, but with the profound understanding of facing and triumphing over blindness and an unthinkable tragedy.

PART I

MY STORY

1

A New World

It was 1964 in my hometown of La Paz, Bolivia, and I was twelve years old. I was with my brother Ed, who was eleven, in the back seat of a 1949 Willis Overland jeep, the family's only form of transportation. Lacking the funds to purchase anything else, my father had refurbished it. Very creatively, he had rebuilt the engine and put together an enclosure made out of wood panels for this old military jeep.

At that time in Bolivia there were no luxuries such as television sets. Consequently, a ride into the downtown area of La Paz in this jeep was an absolute treat for my brother and me as we sat in our "luxury" vehicle, both of us with rosy cheeks. The cold air of the highest capital of the world caused our cheeks to be perennially red; sometimes the cold was so intense that they would crack. All kids had the same problem. It was common and overlooked.

Ed was my worst enemy at that time. We fought constantly so we made sure that each of us stayed as far away from each other as possible. In order to make sure, we sat close to our own windows in the back seat, entertained by the action in the streets.

My feelings during that ride, however, were a mixture of apprehension, embarrassment, and, at the same time, a trace of excitement. My parents sat in the front while my father drove up and down the crowded streets of La Paz, playing a song over and over through a loud speaker he had carefully placed on top of the jeep. The record's lyrics echoed the clamor of Bolivia's citizens to regain the outlet to the sea. This was a very emotional issue for many. The song caused interest among those who felt patriotic enough to have a copy of it. Some would stop their transactions with the vendors who lined the sidewalks and look at us with curiosity. Others paid no attention at all. Those that did approach the window inquired about the song, expressed their enjoyment of it and purchased a record. A few who knew my parents said that they would like a copy but didn't have the money at that time. My father handed them a record but seldom saw the fulfillment of their commitment to pay. This unique way to make some money was not a common practice. It was, however, a very ingenious way for my father to earn the last amount of funds needed to begin his venture to the United States.

My father's efforts paid off. He added the profits of this sale to what we already had, and it was enough to satisfy the demands of the United States Department of Immigration. The requirements for anyone wishing to enter the U.S. and establish permanent residency were stringent to meet. The plan was for him to reach St. Louis, Missouri, find a job, earn enough to rent a place for the family to live, buy some necessary furniture, purchase a car and then send for my mother, my brother, and me. In spite of many friends and family's emphatic admonition about the risky and uncertain future in a foreign country, my father left Bolivia in May 1964, determined to begin a more promising way of life for our family. The struggles he faced, beginning with his inability to speak English, the drastic change of the weather, the unfamiliar culture and intense loneliness were overcome by his tenacious determination. He managed to reach all the goals he had set in just eight short months.

In the meantime, while waiting in Bolivia, my mother's excitement increased. She had read Mark Twain's books about Tom Sawyer's adventures on the Mississippi River. The idea of settling in a city that would bring her close to the places and adventures described in these books added to the anticipation of living in this new land.

The long-awaited day arrived on December 11, 1964. My mom, my brother and I headed to La Paz's airport to board the airplane that would take us to reunite with my father. He anxiously waited for us in St. Louis.

The car pulled away from our house. I glanced out the window and I saw Señora Sanjines as always, standing outside in front of her house on the corner. Her hair was a variety of colors, red, dark brown, light brown; as if she was still in the process of testing the shades before she made up her mind. She would talk to anyone who would listen. Actually she wouldn't just talk; she would complain to herself or to anyone around about everything—her daughter's divorce, her misbehaving grandchildren, etc. Her husband had passed away, so she wore black as a sign of mourning. But I imagine she chose to mourn longer than the usual three-month period—her husband had died years ago. The white, wrinkled, and slightly used handkerchief sticking out of her sweater's sleeve was even more noticeable in her all black attire. From the worn out black high heels, thick black stockings, and old black skirt to the black sweater that was two sizes too small.

She, as well as other neighbors who would stand in front of their homes and visit with one another, was part of the familiar scenery. It also included the vendors seated on specific corners. They were dressed with the colorful but faded clothing, different from that of the middle class. They sat patiently on the ground hoping for a sale of their goods. The supply was limited. It ranged from a few fruits to some candy and loafs of unwrapped bread. These were randomly arranged on top of old cardboard boxes. I knew all their names and even knew some details about their sad stories.

We turned the corner and I distinctly remember looking out the back window of the car at all I was leaving behind. I thought that perhaps I would never see it again. Even at twelve, I realized that this trip was permanent and I attempted to memorize the streets, the various structures, and the familiar scenes. I wanted to hold on to them and never forget them.

If you would ask my mom what she remembered about La Paz, she probably would say the beautiful mountains that surrounded the city. Some of the mountain tops were covered with snow all year long. This panorama made for breathtaking postcards. She also would mention the blue skies, bluer than any other part of the world. She would relate how the stars at night looked so close as if you could almost touch them!

This is what she would probably say, but not me...I remembered the other stuff, like the streets in the area where I lived, which were mostly dirt roads, narrow and hilly, with no sidewalks. Some were cobblestone, but only the main ones were paved. The houses were different in size, structure and design, but they were attached to one another by a common wall between them. For protection, each one had a short wall in front with a door in the middle. It provided access to the front patio that led to the actual entrance of the house. Around the corner from my house was a tall three-story apartment building. I spent a good amount of time inside this building because my two best friends lived there: Jenny on the first floor and Teresa on the second. This structure stood out from the rest because it was painted bright pink. I thought it was pretty; it was new and the color was a drastic contrast to the rest of the houses, which had a drab look to them resembling mud or dirty stucco. Across the street there was a one-story clothing factory and, just like every other structure, a protective cement wall surrounded it. All along the top of these long walls, there were mounds of broken glass glued on with cement. The glass kept intruders from climbing over the wall.

Across from the factory was a public school that had opened up shortly before our departure. In the back of this school building there was an empty and uneven lot, full of weeds and rocks. But this was not an ordinary lot. In one corner where two mud walls met was a home. This homeless person had "built" her residence there. The material? Cardboard and newspapers. Outside this makeshift home were her treasured belongings, some bent, rusty pots, and a collection of dirty and worn out items that she found in the dump located nearby. It was her territory; she tacitly claimed it and no one bothered her. She had a sense of mystery about her. She was mysterious because she never said a word to anyone and seldom left her area. She looked strange—dirty, ragged, hair uncombed and in strands caked with clumps of unknown dirt. Yet, she seemed content just sitting inside her "home." One glance at her as she moved about slowly around her primitive quarters painted a picture of tangible despair, sadness, gloom, and the epitome of poverty.

There was a part of this empty lot, one that was flatter than the rest; that was the best and most enjoyable playground in the world. It consisted of a monkey bar, a swing, and a slide. The latter was anything but sturdy, and it had rough edges and rust spots. The rope holding the swing was worn out as if a mouse had climbed them and taken bites out of it. But they still did the job—they held the only swing in that playground. The board at the end of these two ropes provided frequent enjoyment and at times pain. The piece of wood had weathered and splinters often became cruel reminders that sliding off of it was not a good idea. We never gave a second thought to the condition of the playground.

We just had fun.

Seated in the back of the car, I silently turned to look out of the rear window, attempting to take in all the details of that familiar scene. Maybe it was not pretty, but it was all I knew, it was home, and I felt secure in it. I glanced at the swing; it was swaying with the wind as if waving goodbye to me. Everything else was still, perhaps the neighborhood was also sad to see us go. I took a long look, as long as I could. I took it all in, said a silent good-bye and placed that scene in the files of my memory.

The sadness of leaving my grandparents, particularly my grandmother, was intense and emotionally painful. My mind held the image of her kneeling with rosary in hand, praying for us. Her tender disposition and sweetness touched my heart and I was already missing her! I would always remember her going about her routine, trimming her rose bushes, working in the garden, feeding the birds, reading her Bible, and always having loving and tender words to say anytime Ed and I were around her. I also remember her generous demeanor. On a regular basis, she would prepare a big pot of soup or stew. This meal was not for the family but for those whom she referred to as "the poor." While the dogs barked furiously at those gathered outside the large gate of our home, my grandmother did her thing. She stepped outside the gate and stood in front of those poor souls seated on the ground, looking up and patiently waiting for their much sought-after meal. They resembled the woman who lived in the corner of that lot nearby.

With her big pot of food next to her, my grandmother proceeded to take her large ladle and fill each dingy and shapeless tin bowl. They didn't say much, but the look in their eyes expressed a pitiful but desperate "Thank you!"

My mom, my brother, and I were on the way to a new country where this scenario was rare. The trip was not easy. Travel in small airplanes in those days was not smooth, and my mother and brother suffered the effects of nausea. They made frequent use of the bags available to those passengers who suffered from such a rough plane ride. My brother was so ill that when we finally arrived in the St. Louis airport, he still needed to make urgent trips to the bathroom. But not me—I was too busy looking with amazement at every detail of the airplane. Perhaps I overlooked what was going on in my stomach because I was distracted beyond words by the whole experience, from the plane to the airport to the ride through the new city. My attention was fixed on other strange things that I had never seen before.

The escalators mesmerized me. I had never seen stairways that moved! "Hold on tightly here," my mom instructed me as she took my hand and placed it on the black moving banister. My astonishment quickly turned to fear and apprehension at the thought that I was actually expected to step on one of these stairs still in motion! Little did I know that this would only be the first of many fears that I would be expected to conquer much faster than my young heart and mind could handle.

We exited the airport and headed to the parking lot where the green 1964 Volkswagen Bug waited for us. Wow! A brand new car! Actually for me, everything around me was brand new. This was not a dream, but an exciting reality as this little green bug was transporting the four of us to begin our life in a brand new world!

Rather than a leisurely ride through the city of St. Louis, this trip had to be made with a certain sense of urgency and speed. My brother was still quite ill from the plane ride. In spite of all of this, my father continued enthusiastically to explain the new surroundings as we traveled through the clean St. Louis streets.

"Where are all the people?" I asked with curiosity. The streets of La Paz were constantly crowded with people and vendors lining the sidewalks. It was seldom that anyone should see streets that were empty. For this reason, this desolate appearance of the St. Louis streets amazed me. It seemed so strange to see them so clean...clean as if someone had swept the people away, too!

"It's winter time. Everyone is inside," was my father's logical answer. We continued on through the impressive highways of what would be my hometown for the next thirty-five years. As if watching a movie, we gazed with awe at the drastic difference in the streets, building structures, road systems, and fast highways. Everything seemed like a dream in this New World. Even the method of traffic control was to be admired. As a police officer stopped our car, my father continued to praise the efficient way in which the police force monitored the traffic. He had approached the window and proceeded to inspect my father's driver's license. Communicating with gestures, he thanked the officer. It wasn't until weeks later that, after talking to new acquaintances, we learned that what we had received from the police officer was a speeding ticket!

Learning the Hard Way

Job-hunting for my parents was not easy, but their determination to persevere and their humility were the characteristics that brought them to success. My father began to work for a large hotel unloading produce from trucks. Unable to speak English, this type of work was the only one he could obtain. He persevered through moments of humiliation. At times he was misunderstood or, even worse, he did not fully understand simple instructions from his supervisors. The result was that he was the object of embarrassing scolding. He swallowed his pride and continued on. Eventually, he moved up in positions. Once he gained a more fluent command of the language, he looked for work in the field he was involved with, in Bolivia, the recording industry. Through the years that followed, he moved on but always to better jobs. The last position he held was in the exporting department of a large chemical company. His ability to speak Spanish came in handy. His duties included communications with South American countries regarding the exportation of pharmaceutical chemicals. He ended up retiring from this company with full benefits and pension.

My mom had some training in Library Science in Bolivia. Two months after arriving in St. Louis, she saw an ad in the newspaper for work in a library-related clerical position. The job opening was for the Instructional Resources Department of a local community college. She promptly applied. During the interview, she quickly recognized that there would be no hope of getting the position—she could not understand all the questions posed to her by her interviewer; much less give an impressive answer. My mom's solution was to make an offer, with a pleading tone, to the American lady, "I work one day. You like, you pay. You no like my work; you don't pay." Perhaps it was compassion that prompted this interviewer to accept my mom's proposal. She sat my mom at a typewriter and asked her to draft a letter. More nervous than before, my mom, who had always used manual typewriters, pressed a key once and, to her surprise and shock, she saw how the paper reflected a full row of that same letter. She soon learned that the keys in electric typewriters are much more sensitive than those of a manual! She regained her composure somehow. Not knowing how to begin the letter, she scrambled to find a format to use as a guide. She searched through the waste paper basket next to a desk, pulled out a letter, and followed its format.

The letter must have been acceptable because she was asked to come back the next day. That next day was the beginning of my mom's career of twenty-one years. She held a variety of positions with the St. Louis Community College, and I am still in awe at the fluency she gained with the English language. Although she speaks with an accent, her grammar, sentence structure, and command of English are admirable. She retired with many commendations for her work. She was admired for her unequaled traits, punctuality, dedication, and diligence. She was also regarded as the "light that brought joy to all those who worked with her."

Nightmare

My father believed in overcoming any difficulty by facing and dealing with it. He made it very clear that he wished for this determination to be instilled in my brother and me. Consequently, he enrolled us in St. Roch's school, which was close to our apartment. Two days after our arrival, and before we could adjust to anything, we were off to our first day in the new school. The only way to describe this day is as an unwanted nightmare for me. Unable to understand a word of English, the utterances made by the teacher and students were nothing more than incomprehensible noises. This only added to my feeling of confusion and fear. On the first day I found myself surrounded by a group of sixth-grade girls who were laughing and whispering. It wasn't necessary for me to understand the words they said because it was clear to me that they found something amusing and unusual about me. This unwanted attention just increased my feeling of humiliation and desperation. I found out later that they couldn't believe that I had my ears pierced. In 1964, this was not a common practice in the United States, but it was common for most Bolivian parents to take their month-old girls to have their ears pierced.

Another episode I remember from those early school days was when a note was sent home from school indicating that the gym uniform should be a pair of shorts worn together with the uniform blouse. My mom made efforts to make sense of the note with the aid of a dictionary. She learned that "shorts" were a pants-like garment worn above the knees. She proceeded to take me to Sears and buy me the "shorts" I needed to wear under my uniform. The laughter and ridicule I heard from the classmates when I took my uniform off in gym class will be one that I shall never forget. As they all formed a line wearing their stylish navy blue gym shorts, I stood out like a sore thumb—my mom had bought me blue and green striped bloomers!

Among the difficult and embarrassing moments, however, there were also comforting experiences. I managed to make friends, ones who accepted me just the way I was. We got to know each other as we walked to and from school every day. Not only did I enjoy their company, but also our interaction helped to improve my ability to speak English. I was grateful for their patience and acceptance in spite of my accent, as well as my lack of knowledge of the games and ways of the American culture. It didn't take long before I felt comfortable with them and looked forward to the opportunities to participate in the variety of activities we did together.

Soon after we arrived in St. Louis I was assigned the job of starting dinner when I came home from school. I learned to cook with my mom's careful instructions. Cooking, however, was not as tedious as it could have been for me at thirteen. It actually became an activity that I enjoyed along with my new American friends. For some reason, they chose to help me, so we would step in my kitchen and together prepare basic dishes, ones that my Mom would finish when she got home from work.

I imagine there were some things they learned from me, but I also learned a lot from them. In Bolivia, nothing came pre-mixed; everything had to be made from scratch. I stood in amazement as my friend's mom simply opened a box of cake mix, added an egg, some oil, mixed, and baked it! The result was an actual cake and more delicious than the ones I had ever tasted.

I cherish the memories of those friends. We became very close; in fact, I still enjoy keeping in contact with some of them as we reminisce about our times together so long ago.

2

Unwelcome News

As difficult as adjusting to our new land and home was, before long I faced an unexpected adjustment that had nothing to do with the culture. As we began our new American way of life, including good medical care, my father noticed some trouble with his eyesight. After the routine exam of an ophthalmologist, he learned that he suffered from a disease called Retinitis Pigmentosa (RP). This disease affects the retina of the eye, causing it to deteriorate. In 1965, this disease was difficult to diagnose in the patients who suffered from it. It was still foreign to the medical profession. The doctor informed us that there was no cure for this disease and could possibly, with time, cause blindness. We further learned that it was hereditary.

My brother's retina seemed to be perfectly healthy; however, I showed signs of having the disease. Although the doctor mentioned that night blindness was one of the first symptoms I might expect, he assured us that we probably would not see any significant changes in my eyesight until the age of sixty. The medical profession did not know what aggravated the condition, or what one could do to prevent it.

(At the time of this writing there is still no cure, surgery, medication, or transplant available to patients who have lost their sight to this disease). The ophthalmologist's diagnosis explained the difficulties I was already experiencing. However, for some reason I, at that young age, had never been aware that my vision at night was different from anyone else's. I assumed everyone must have the same difficulty seeing at night as I did.

The newly acquired information about RP did not cause any apparent concern for my family or me. Life went on. The neighborhood where my father had chosen for us to live was quickly deteriorating, so we moved to a different part of town. My brother and I were enrolled in St. Mary Magdalen School. I attended eighth grade there, and then went on to Bishop DuBourg High School. There are many reasons why I hold good memories of those years. By this time, I had gained confidence and began to feel more comfortable with my new life in the United States.

As I continued to gain fluency in English, I began to put more trust in my own abilities. Learning to face difficult situations and overcoming them developed a determination in my character that helped me to do well academically. I took pride in consistently making the honor roll, as well as in participating in extracurricular activities.

One of the more enjoyable events for my friends and me was to attend the dances held at the gymnasium of the school. Unfortunately, my enjoyment was dampened by a certain sense of apprehension on my part. I was unable to navigate in dimly lit areas. I had to depend on my friends' patient assistance.

Everyone has a most embarrassing moment, one that we try to forget. Mine came on the dance floor. I imagine the teenage years are more sensitive and, while hormones are ruling the emotions, somehow everything seems more traumatic. I was no exception and thus saw myself as a victim of this painful stage of life. For us girls in the freshman year of high school, it was the not-so-hidden desire to "be asked to dance" by any of the nice looking boys. When one of the most popular ones asked me to dance, it seemed as if my heart beat a little faster with excitement.

My way of coping with my lack of vision in this dark dance hall was to "pretend" that I could see as well as everyone else. After a few minutes, the band was still playing a great dancing song. As I tried hard to make sure I did all the "cool" dance moves, I had not noticed that I eventually ended up with my back to him during the whole song. One of my friends came and gave me the painful news of why I was being laughed at. Sometimes laughter can be the cruelest weapon one can be the victim of. But all I could do was to laugh with them, even though inside I was mortified and was sobbing.

There was no hope of running and hiding—it was too dark for me to run on my own! You guessed it! He never asked me to dance again! It took me a long time to have the courage to accept an invitation to dance from any young man. With time, however, my passion for dancing won over the embarrassment I suffered, especially if I wanted to continue dancing. My night blindness could not be resolved, so I had to somehow come to terms with that fact. Although reluctantly, I was forced to accept it, adjust to it, and try to move on.

3

College Life

By this time I had gone through a lot in my life that had helped build my character and should have built my self-confidence. But for some reason, I still had feelings of unnecessary apprehensions when I faced new situations, such as going away to school. I attended a local community college in St. Louis for the first two years. Upon graduation, one of my dearest friends, Marty, and I decided to continue college together, and we transferred to a four-year university. The decision was fully supported by my parents, for they felt that my brother and I should take advantage of all the education opportunities available to us.

The adjustment to a college life away from home was not easy for me. I still cannot pinpoint the reason why, but dorm life in a college located two hours away from my family was traumatic. I remember calling home with a trembling voice, trying hard to hold back the tears just to say what I was supposed to say…that everything was fine. I didn't dare say what my heart really felt. Just as before, I was expected to adjust and make the best of whatever situation I found myself in. "Adjustments" should have been a way of life for me. I had been forced to do so from the moment we set foot in the St. Louis airport. I should have been a master at this by now. It was not so for I missed my family and the security of my parent's guidelines. Strangely enough, they provided a hidden sense of protection for me.

My roommate Marty, as well as the other college girls in the dorm, seemed to enjoy college life. For some of them it brought the freedom they longed for. I never could identify with this view of independence they held. Unlike me, they did have the full independence college life offered them, while I was still very apprehensive about my visual limitations at night. I made sure not to sign up for classes at night. I found any excuse not to commit to school activities that required me to walk around the campus while it was dark.

Since I wasn't qualified as a "handicapped" student, there were no special provisions made for me—nor did I request any. I continued on just like everyone else. When needed, I sought the assistance of my friends. My main focus was on spending enough time studying in order to get consistently good grades.

Although I never adjusted to college life, I did overcome the feelings of homesickness and decided to enjoy my days as much as I could.

"Don't tell me Jan. You have another date tonight?" asked one of the girls in the dorm with disbelief and a tone of jealousy. I had other dates on that same weekend, and I imagined that she felt I had more than my share. My social activities at night around campus always had to include the company of someone. There never seemed to be a lack of young men who gladly offered to do so, although this wasn't always a good thing.

Those ladies reading my story will identify with this. Did you ever accept a date with a guy and thought you made a good choice, only to find out that you had made a big mistake? I did that very thing. I would at times accept an invitation from what seemed to be a promising nice and pleasant date. Sadly enough, after a few moments into the evening, the disappointment crept in. He wouldn't be nearly as "cool" as I thought, and as the evening progressed, it would turn from pleasant into a long nightmare. Most girls could make the best of it by avoiding "hanging on him," either holding his hand or arm. In my case, however, I had no choice but to hold his hand and hang on to him for dear life. Not doing so would mean that I would run into objects, people or fall down steps. Anyone observing us possibly would think that I was crazy about him by the way I hung on to his hand with what would seem to others a sign of affection!   And often, the young man took it this way as well.

I had accepted a date with a guy named Tony. He seemed like an ok guy, but what was attractive to me was the activity he had planned for the date—sailing. He had a sailboat, and we were going to enjoy an afternoon along with another couple. We arrived at a lake located two hours away. I was glad that these friends went with us because I didn't know Tony too well, and I felt more comfortable in a group. We all headed for the boat, but to my surprise, the other couple decided to do something else at the last minute.

"Are you ready, babe?" Tony said to me.

"Babe?" I thought with annoyance. "Where did he get that from?"

I barely knew him and I did not appreciate this familiar endearment term he was using with me. I ignored it and followed him to this new little adventure. As Tony and I got into the sailboat, I had an uneasy feeling—this sort of strange guy and me in the middle of a large lake. Before I knew it, we had sailed to the middle of the lake. The weather was pleasant...but not my date. I soon learned that he liked to fish—the bait he used? The sailboat. The catch of the day? Me! The instant he made the first inappropriate move, he was met with my assertive, clear, and loud, "Stop!" He got the message…there is nothing more unattractive than a man who pouts. The sail back to shore was silent, with each of us at opposite ends of the sailboat!

I didn't realize it then, but this steady dating was more than just an enjoyment. This stage of life brings to light some insecurities not identified before. I had other needs that were subtler than the need to have someone to spend time with. I know now that it was a way to cover up what I seemed to lack inside my heart. I had a void and longed to fill it. I attempted to do so with the sense of comfort I obtained from the attention of the opposite sex. This might have been the reason why I also hung on to a boyfriend who was back home. He remained in the background for some years while I "played the field" in my days away at college.

Perhaps I wasn't alone in this subtle search for fulfill-ment. Other coeds might have also been looking to fill a void just like I was. I imagine that some found it in drinking, others in drugs, yet others in healthier activities such as sports. But I looked for it in yet another way. I found it in dating. Dating back then was quite different than it is now. For me, the process was clearly defined because I was selec-tive in accepting dates with young men. An occasional good night kiss when they took me back to the dorm was the limit of any expression of affection.

In addition to dating, I enjoyed the company of my dear friends, who remained faithful in their assistance whenever I needed it. Those years were the 70s, which brought with it a craze for disco dancing. My friends and I would enjoy dancing at discotheques. Since most of them were dimly lit and too dark for me to see anything clearly, we developed a code whereby one of them would discreetly whisper a phrase to me that would tell me if I should accept the young man's invitation to dance or not. This worked quite well since my friends' taste in men was the same as mine.

My college life was not only providing an education in

academics but in life itself. Some of these lessons were learned the hard way. Believing that I was in love, I accepted a marriage proposal from the boyfriend back home. The mistake on both of our parts was evident when we, as was typical of our relationship, entered into a heated quarrel, and we both agreed to end the engagement after one week. But what was more indicative of our emotional immaturity was that this "break up" took place in the middle of our engagement party, a gathering that was so kindly planned for us by our close friends.

Two weeks after this disastrous break-up, I went back to attend my last semester at college. "Jan, I heard what happened at your engagement party!" exclaimed a friend who lived in the same dorm.

"Boy! News travels fast," I said with a tone of surprise and at the same time with a hint of embarrassment.

Ignoring my reaction and without hesitation, she proceeded to tell me about a guy who happened to be her boyfriend's roommate. "He has the most beautiful blue eyes!" she informed me. "How about going to Saturday night's 50s dance with him?"

Go out with another guy? I thought, I need some time to think things over. After all I had just gone through an unpleasant engagement break-up. But I imagine that the time I needed was shorter than I thought. With little enthusiasm, I said, "OK, but I need to meet him and get to know him a little first. I don't want to go to a dance with someone I just met." She agreed.

The blue-eyed young man who called me that very night was Gene Eckles. I don't think that it was love at first sight. However, there was definitely a strong attraction between the two of us. When he called me and asked me out on a date, I accepted. We hit it off just fine, so he asked me out the next night...and the next...and the next one as well! I didn't refuse and was happy to spend time with him.

Gene was sensitive, sweet, and handsome. I informed him that I would need assistance in walking if we were to be anywhere with dim lighting. As most young men I dated, he was very understanding and accommodating. Among all of them, however, Gene was different in many ways. I liked the way he listened. I love to talk. When I talked to him, he proved to be a good listener, a trait that was not common among the college men I knew.

Coincidentally he happened to be twelve hours older than I was. We realized that our moms were in labor simultaneously, his in St. Louis, Missouri, and mine in La Paz, Bolivia. As soon as I found that we were so close in age, I began to go into the common horoscope signs, which I thought united us…we were both Scorpios. Since I was still living much in the world's values guided by astrology and horoscope signs, I felt that our relationship was meant to be. I talked to him about this wonderful and not-so-coincidental fact about us and shared with him my views about this belief.

He also stood out to me in other ways. Gene belonged to the business fraternity for men, and I belonged to the woman's business sorority. Consequently, we attended many events, which included drinking and somewhat wild behavior for that time period. It was at these events where I noticed that Gene was different from the rest. He would not indulge in drinking or immature behavior. His gentle and sensible demeanor drew me to him as I admired his sense of self-control. He didn't attempt to "fit in" with the rest. On the contrary, I seemed to be more important to him than what other people might think of him—or me! He would make efforts to make me feel special and respected.

Soon we stopped attending these events and chose to spend time with each other. I do admit he was a distraction to my study time, but, fortunately, I was a positive influence on him. As I spent time in the library studying, he also had no choice but to open his books and study alongside me. His grades improved, and he graduated Summa Cum Laude and later obtained his CPA certification. Even to this day, our college friends remind us that I was a good influence on him—I find that it was a mutual effort.

Looking at our horoscopes and common grounds, we concluded that fate must have brought us together. That was our conclusion then. It was only later, when I realized how much and how often God had His hand on my life, did I realize that there is no such thing as "fate." There is only a perfect plan molded by God.

4

Happily Ever After

Gene possessed other qualities that I had not found in other men; ones that I was particularly attracted to. He displayed a more mature demeanor as well as an ability to communicate with the eloquence not typical of men his age. He became very special to me. We dated exclusively, and while still in my senior year in college, we became engaged. My parents discreetly showed their understandable surprise. I am sure that my recent engagement to someone else was fresh in their minds. Nevertheless, they expressed their hesitant, but supportive approval. Gene and I planned our wedding for the following year. We focused on coordinating the details of that important event in our lives.

Among the steps we took to prepare for our marriage, I thought we should include one, which most engaged couples don't have to take. I felt strongly that Gene should know the prognosis of the retinal disease, as well as the possible effects on our children if we were to have some in the future. We made an appointment with the ophthalmologist in order to learn more about what to expect.

If there were ever a time when I could pinpoint the beginning of my maturity into adulthood, it would be at that moment sitting across the desk of that ophthalmologist. I learned for the first time what life could bring—coldness and cruelty. Gene and I stepped into the spacious office of the only ophthalmologist in the area who was familiar with RP.

"Sit down," he offered, with a tone lacking friendliness. He must have been used to these types of visits; giving bad news to his patients must not have been pleasant for him. "I guess you know that the results show that there is no doubt that you as well as your father have RP."

"Yes, we know," I responded with a sad tone.

Gene spoke up, "Is there any danger of this being passed on to our children?" He was curious but had a hint of hope in his voice that we would receive a negative answer.

The doctor, however, was not encouraging. "We don't know, there are so many types of RP, no one can tell for sure. But there might be a 50 percent chance of your children inheriting the RP gene."

"Is there anything that you know of anywhere which could prevent the loss of sight or at least prolong it?" I asked with desperation difficult to hide.

"Well, you can be crazy, like that guy who went to Russia and got needles stuck in his eyeballs...all he got was a serious infection. There are all kinds of quacks all over promising you a cure." He continued with little empathy. "If there is a treatment or cure, you'll hear it before me—it will be all over the news." He added with a sarcastic chuckle. "I must warn you that I would consider adoption."

He stood up as he hit us with this final bit of information. Perhaps he didn't want to see me cry and make a scene, but I refused to let all my feelings out in front of this man who seemed to be insensitive and cold. My judgment of his attitude was probably a result of my emotional state. In reality he wasn't all that cold. He simply had nothing else to say or offer to us.

His friendly nurse confirmed this. "There's no need to make a follow-up appointment."

Of course not, there was nothing that could be done—it would be just a matter of time.

"We'll be okay," said Gene in a soft voice. He held onto me as we walked out of that sentencing chamber. His comfort and reassurances made me love him all the more.

The tears I shed on that day were the first of many as a result of being afflicted by this disease. I found it extremely difficult to accept that my lifelong desire to be a mom was being taken away.

Although we both felt the same disappointment, we chose to disregard the ophthalmologist's admonition and decided to go on with our lives. I was determined to focus on the reality given by the initial doctor, who had affirmed years ago that I would not see any effect in my eyesight until the age of sixty. Therefore, any concern or fear regarding RP was quickly dismissed and forgotten.

After a one-year engagement, Gene and I were married. We rented a small two-bedroom apartment close to the neighborhood I lived. No frills, simple; the rent was $145 a month, but I guess you get what you pay for. What I remember most is that it had bright royal blue carpeting throughout. The popular colors at that time were a combination of yellow, orange, and brown. The couch we bought was a blend of these exact colors. When we placed it on top of that blue carpet, it would undoubtedly have caused a shriek of horror from any professional decorator.

But as the carpet's color clashed with that of our furniture, so did Gene's and my way of life. We had unrealistically expected to begin a married life full of happiness and satisfaction. But the reality was not so. At twenty-three years of age, Gene and I focused on the details of preparing the wedding day. As most couples, we did not spend enough time and effort in preparing for the marriage. As a result, our first year as husband and wife was a painful adjustment and at times our days together were unbearable. We both brought to the relationship a series of unresolved issues. We had been exposed to opposing family values. We had negative childhood experiences, priorities, individual desires, goals, and unrealistic expectations.

Although home from college and attending church once again, I held no spiritual convictions applicable to my life. Therefore, as I look back, I believe wholeheartedly that it was our parents' prayers that somehow helped Gene and me to survive that first dreadful year. It wasn't until much later that I could see that this period of time was a painful but necessary experience for us. The years that followed seemed easier as we took steps to successfully go through the adjustment stages of our marriage.

5

My World Closing In

A year and a half after we were married, Gene graduated from college with an accounting degree, and he
accepted a position with a national accounting firm in St.
Louis. A year later, our first son Jason was born. He was our
delight and the object of doting grandparents. He grew
quickly—too quickly. Before we knew it he was walking and
all too soon, he had his second birthday.

It was an autumn day in St. Louis. The colors of the
leaves on the trees were changing along with the temperature. It was cool outside so I grabbed a sweater. It looked
anything but stylish because I couldn't button it. I was seven
months pregnant with our son Jeff. After giving the necessary instructions to the babysitter who would care for Jason,
I left the house feeling unattractive and frumpy. I was
headed to my yearly eye check-up. I was headed to the eye
doctor's office for a simple and routine visit. Fortunately I
had not noticed any changes in my vision. I reached the doctor's office building, took the elevator to his suite, and found
a seat in the waiting room. My turn came and I was called to
his small but well-equipped office. There I sat in front of the

familiar device designed with a chin rest. "Look straight ahead," he said, with a less-than-cordial tone.

"Hmm…How did you get here?" he asked, with a tone of curiosity as he examined the back of my eye shining a light through my dilated pupils. "I drove myself," I replied, somewhat perplexed at his question. He uttered a sound of surprise and dismissed the subject. One week later on October 27, the very same day that I turned 27, my birthday celebration was slightly dampened. I received a letter from him, informing me that it was his professional opinion that I discontinue the operation of any motor vehicle. He expanded by indicating that the deterioration of my eyesight made this practice very dangerous.

My initial reaction was that of anger and frustration mixed with fear. I quickly found comfort and reassurance by remembering the words from the ophthalmologist who had diagnosed me when I was thirteen, and said I would be sixty before I noticed any changes—I had a long way to go! I rationalized that I was very much in control. I knew all too well of my limitations of driving at night; consequently, I avoided doing so. I felt confident in my driving abilities during the day. I quickly tore up the letter and decided not to share those unpleasant warnings with anyone.

Life went on as we were blessed with the birth of our second son Jeff, and our joy increased as our family grew with yet another addition, Joe, who was born eighteen months later. I felt very grateful that Gene's career provided for our family, and I was able to stay home and care for our three sons.

Our future looked bright and promising. We all have points of references when we choose our goals. As Gene worked for a large accounting firm, we attended fancy parties in homes of those who had climbed the ladder. I secretly hoped that Gene would some day reach that level, and we would end up in a similar home, with expensive furniture and fancy gadgets. I could still see then, and I never missed the opportunity to analyze the kind of appearance one should have to portray a certain "look." I was definitely caught up with the desire to possess name brand and designer labels, ones we could not really afford yet. At this stage of our lives, they were all still just dreams. I was driven by the sense of finding fulfillment by the possession of material things.

In the meantime, our days were filled with the consuming tasks of caring for our small sons. The fact that I couldn't drive at night didn't cause any serious problems for the family. Gene made sure that he was always available. Knowing that he was patiently willing to take over, reassured me and made my job easier. Time seemed to pass quickly. The boys were now a little older, and we celebrated the stage of life that seemed to never come, all three boys were out of diapers!

By that time, Gene and I had been married for about eight years and our life was very busy. Like many American parents, we were focused on providing our sons every opportunity to enjoy as much as they could in life. As a result, we were part of the endless routine of going from one activity to another.

Our mornings began with exhaustion. We weren't among those lucky parents whose children slept through the night. I think they were in first grade before they each slept all night through. Maybe it wasn't that long, but it sure seemed like it. Gene and I did everything we could to get them to sleep all night long. Jason would come in our room so often that we decided to put a mattress next to our bed. Then when Jeff got up, we would put him next to Jason. Joe was the one who ended up with us in bed. I sometimes wondered if we were just as active at night trying to juggle our three little J's.

The next day always came too soon. Gene would somehow gather enough energy in the mornings to make it through his day at work. What got me through my day was the hope of lying down while they took a nap. Unfortunately, it remained just a hope since they didn't take naps all at the same time.

My job as a typical mom included driving them to countless sport activities, Boy Scout events, social functions, and other events. My emotions as a mom were varied. They included happiness, satisfaction; a sense of reward and at times concern. I worried about meeting the demands of my family adequately. These emotions certainly did not include any concern regarding my own health.

Along with the goal to become the best mom I could, I had specific personal dreams as well. It was the end of the 70s and the feminist movement was at its prime. Stay-at-home moms seemed to have lost their confidence. The popular way of thinking prevailed. It echoed a shallow view indicating that women at home caring for their children were "missing out" on the benefits brought to them by climbing the corporate ladder. The erroneous clamor was that women live up to their potential only when seeking out professional success.

My heart held contrary views. I believed that women could reach more success than any CEO by devoting the prime of their lives caring for and raising children. This is a most demanding, challenging as well as rewarding task for any woman anywhere.

I became active in the effort to change this destructive feminist view. I volunteered for a non-profit organization called Mother's Center. It had become a routine for me to pack my three little bundles in their car seats in the morning and, for a couple of hours, dedicate my efforts to this cause. I facilitated groups for other mothers who, like me, needed the emotional support in the job as stay-at-home moms. When it was convenient for the schedule of our three small sons, I accepted opportunities to give interviews for radio stations, local TV talk shows, and print publications, such as the interview I did with *American Baby* in New York. I was outspoken as I offered support to those moms being bombarded by misguided views of the most valuable gift of motherhood.

Everything for our family was taking place just as planned. We were living out the dream Gene and I had. He was climbing up the corporate ladder quickly, our sons were healthy and I was able to stay home to care for them. What was about to happen, however, did not fit into the plans Gene and I had. As adverse events in life show up often without advance notice, catching us unprepared, we were about to face something undeserved. This blow seemed to just hit us so unexpectedly at a time when our focus was on the positive and promising aspect of life. We were caught off-guard and unequipped to handle the reality of losing my sight so soon. I had been wrong in trusting the prognosis the first ophthalmologist had given me long ago.

Any crisis that enters our lives without warning brings about emotions difficult to hold back. Terror might be an accurate word to describe my feelings. I began to undeniably experience evidence of losing my eyesight. Initially I told no one about this, but the peripheral field was beginning to diminish in a way that I could not ignore.

The neighbors joked about the fact that I had, for the third time, run into the mailbox located at the end of our driveway. I didn't dare share with anyone that I simply didn't see it. Finally, I confided in Gene that I was only driving in the streets that were familiar to me. There was no reason to be concerned because, luckily, I had not been involved in any accidents. I knew, however, that it was just a matter of time before something tragic would happen.

The most frightening situation for me was while I was driving the car. Our three small sons in the back seat would display their active nature as only a seven, five, and three year old could. Maintaining the concentration needed for me to drive safely became an arduous struggle. I realized the risk I was taking as I sensed that my vision was not able to take in enough of the road to see the cars coming along side of me. When needed, I began to compensate by moving my head from side to side to increase my field of vision. Subconsciously, I developed a variety of tactics to make up for the decreasing peripheral vision. Eventually, driving became an overwhelming challenge and a source of emotional and physical drain on me. The pride I held inside would not let me admit to myself or to anyone else that I was beginning to lose my sight. Finally, the extreme effort needed to drive a car soon was more than I could handle. The fear of hurting someone or hurting my sons in an accident was what brought me to the painful decision to give up the car keys.

It was a mixture of anger and relief at the same time. At the age of 32, I was, in a sense, giving up my independence before I was ready to do so. Resentment filled my heart because this surrender was not part of my plans. The dreams I had for a fulfilling life were being replaced by a tangible darkness around me. In an effort to find comfort, I rationalized by thinking that there are much worse setbacks in life than the inability to drive. I reasoned that there would be other forms of transportation available for me to continue my active lifestyle. I would somehow be able to find ways for my sons to participate in their activities as before. I was determined to do all I could in order for our lives to remain normal. I had to make sure that I stayed "together" for Gene. He would have his own emotions to deal with. His wife, with no warning, could no longer do her part for the family as before.

Denial and refusal to give in were the order of the day. This was short-lived, however, because it became difficult to deny that my peripheral vision was noticeably closing in. In less than a year, the disease progressed so much so that I began to run into furniture, walls, and trip over items on the floor. My vision soon diminished to the point that I saw my blurry surroundings as if I was looking through a keyhole. This stage of being partially blind is possibly the most difficult for someone losing his or her sight. You continue to trust in the ability to see as before, but lack the ability to navigate using your other senses. At times I would trip over a toy on the floor. When I bent down to pick it up and unable to see the piece of furniture in the way, I would hit my head with a thud causing a deep black and blue bruise. I had not developed ways to use my hands as a guide to prevent such mishaps. This lack of adjustment turned simple tasks such as loading the dishwasher into a somewhat dangerous chore. At times, while loading it I became distracted, a bloody abrasion or scrape on my leg caused by running into the open door would be the painful reminder that I had not closed it.

Not only did I choose to overlook the physical pain, I also chose to ignore the emotional pain Gene and I felt at this particular stage of my blindness. This dismissal of reality created a wall around each of us built by feelings of denial. Lacking any other way to face this ugly monster, perhaps we chose this denial to desperately serve as a safe boundary between us. We both silently believed that this would be a temporary situation and something would take place to fix it so that we could go on as before. I had always been a determined person able to deal with obstacles in creative and effective ways; but this rapid loss of my eyesight was more than I could manage. For the time being, I attempted to do everything possible for our family to continue our routine. As difficult as it was to go forward, I still managed to "cover up" the deficiencies of my diminishing eyesight.

6

Living In Darkness

By the time Jason turned eight, Jeff six, and Joe four, my vision had closed in completely. I was only able to detect the faint glow of a light coming from a window or an artificial light at night. The adjustment for me had begun, but not without the unavoidable emotions of anger and frustration. I chose to focus on simply achieving the activities of the day in the best way that I could. Sometimes, however, that just wasn't sufficient.

Moms have to have eyes even in the back of their heads, right? But when a Mom has no eyes at all with which to see what three active little boys are doing, life becomes more than a bit difficult. My ears became the means by which I could determine what they were up to. So often I would approach the screen door and listen to make sure they were safe and were still in the backyard. All three learned quickly that when I called their names, they should answer right away. I developed a rapid method of tracking them down. I memorized every phone number of the neighbors around our home. They were friends so I felt comfortable checking with them to make sure our sons were there.

I tried hard for our sons to have a "normal" environment at home. Had they watched me suffer, cry, or become angry whenever I ran into something, perhaps they might have learned to fear for me. But they didn't. I didn't let them. As a result, they treated me as if I could see. Jeff seemed to be the most sensitive, when his brothers would run off, he would stay back, "I'll help you, Mommy!" was his tender offer as he took my hand and helped me walk.

The most frightening moment for me was when Joe was five years old. He was racing down hill on a skateboard, but he looked back instead of where he was going. He went right under a parked car across from our house, and put a deep gash in his head. A neighbor brought him home, Joe was screaming like never before. I was frantic because I couldn't see where the blood was coming from. The towels were soaked, but I just could not determine where he was hurt. I felt so helpless and truly inadequate. A neighbor took us to the emergency room and Gene met us there. The ten stitches left a large scar for life. I think the scar left in my heart might have been just as big.

But caring for the boys was not my only struggle. It became more evident for me as well as to family members that I couldn't walk freely or safely around the house anymore. My inability to see where the open spaces or paths to walk through in each room caused me to run into corners of walls, into partially opened doors, or a piece of furniture. Although I learned quickly to concentrate and remember where everything was, often the children would cause a slight distraction and I would run into something with such impact that it would cause the skin to break open. The bleeding more often than not would mix with the tears of physical as well as emotional pain. I chose to put the pain aside in order to move forward with the task that I set out to do. The boys' care was a demanding job and I was determined that no one else would do it but me.

It was frightening and painful to accept the cruel reality that I not only was blind to my surroundings but that I would never again see the smiles on my boys' faces. I would not see the changes that took place as they grew up. I would not watch their skills as they played the various sports or see the expressions on their faces that give a Mom the sign that is needed to know what might be in their hearts.

Sometimes I found myself using every ounce of energy just to overcome the desperate frustration in order to keep going. Each chore around the house had to be learned all over again. For example, the cooking became a painful job at times when I would reach over a little too far and my fingers would catch the burning pot. I was forced to come up with ways to get around this. I found that using a wooden spoon to guide me would minimize the burning. Using the oven was much simpler because thick long oven gloves provided the adequate protection. At times I had mistakenly put flour rather than powdered sugar into a recipe. Other ingredients were simpler to tell apart such as sugar and salt because they were kept in containers quite different from one another. I arranged the groceries in specific places in the pantry, placing rubber bands around certain cans to differentiate cans of soup from the others. I placed the boxes of various items in certain and specific places inside the kitchen cabinets. This way, it was easier for me to "feel" where they were.

My way to find anything around the house was and still is to feel with my hands. When our youngest son Joe was four, he had the ability to express himself very well. He often managed to have an explanation for everything. I overheard him once explain to his friends that his Mom had eyes at the end of her fingers because that's how she sees.

Those "eyes" that Joe told his friends I had at the end of my fingers did not work too well all the time. Ironing was another physically painful chore at first. It took only one time to burn my hand before I decided to reach for the hot iron by following the electric cord leading up to it. This way I was sure to find the handle rather than the hot iron itself. Doing the laundry was not difficult, but separating the white clothing from the others certainly was. As a result I had a higher level of appreciation for Gene's patience, as he never complained about wearing pink underwear! Once the clothes were ready to be put away, I had to find a way to separate them in order to place them in each of the boy's rooms. Their sizes were close to one another so I differentiated them by stapling one staple on the tag of Jeff's shirt, two for Joe, and none for Jason. This made it easier for me to simply feel the tag and determine to whom the shirts belonged. I did the same with their school uniform pants. I placed a staple on the inside of the belt loop.

I found creative ways to perform the household chores. But there was one, which I felt was more important than a chore, but was impossible for me to do: help my sons with their homework. I felt desperate and angry because the printed page soon became a blank piece of nothing, as my eyes could no longer focus on the detail of any object put in front of me. Children seem to have the ability to adjust to situations much easier than adults do. Once our sons knew that their mom couldn't see, they realized that they couldn't "show" me anything. Instead, they became quite skilled in describing what they needed me to "see." It became a way of life for them. However, the more frustrating thing was that, as typical little boys, none of them would volunteer any information they received from their teachers such as a "meet the teacher night," or reminders such as "its picture day tomorrow." As a result, I would make sure that I searched through their book bags and hold on to any wrinkled piece of paper to hand to Gene when he got home from work. Inevitably, when he was out of town for work reasons, we would miss an event; I learned to rely on the kindness of other moms. As they received my phone calls asking for this or that, they were always ready to provide me with clarifications or new information I needed to have.

As if the care of our three small sons wasn't enough, we had also unwisely opened our home to Ramon, a seventeen-year-old exchange student from Spain. We thought he would "help" out with the boys in some form or another. Although our sons enjoyed the company of a temporary big brother, having him live with us for a year at this particular period of time was not the best choice. I had to keep up with the activities and school requirements as parents for him in high school, Jason in grade school, Jeff in kindergarten, and Joe in pre-school. It was difficult for Gene and for me because it seemed as if they, at one time or another, all had events, which needed our attendance and some participation as well.

I missed a lot of things, especially activities with the boys, or the things I enjoyed doing alone. But what I missed most was my independence. I resented the fact that I could no longer jump in the car and take my sons to the countless number of places they needed to go. Nor could I take off to the mall whenever I had the opportunity. Those days were long gone where I could take a look at the newspaper and learn that an item I needed just came on sale. The opportunities for me to go with friends had to understandably be according to their schedule and not mine. Although I was grateful when a friend would invite me, my heart held feelings of jealousy because of the freedom they had and for the independence I had lost.

But this was only a trivial example of the real crisis I was in the middle of. In the big picture, the reluctance to accept my blindness continued to consume me emotionally and spiritually. There were moments when it was more intense than others were. For example, when Gene and I would ride in the car, my inability to see anything out the windows was devastating. I would find myself asking Gene where we were, only to find out that we were in areas that I had frequently driven myself not long ago. Unable to see any images through the windows, the car became a movable but closed-in box with a motor. Similarly, my life now was also somehow moving forward, but it was much like being inside a dark closed-in booth with no openings.

I don't know if it was determination or a survival instinct, but I continued to do most of the chores for the family. Gene did everything else. The grocery shopping was, and continues to be, the chore that I dislike the most, even when someone else is accompanying me. But Gene's patience and devotion to the family seemed to be ever present. He took care of this task in addition to all the driving for the family, paying the bills, paperwork, and shopping. He took the boys to all their numerous activities. But more importantly, he spent time with them, demonstrating constant affection and love for they were and still are the light of our lives. The patience and dedication on Gene's part was consistently demonstrated when he would come home from work drained after a long day, only to find the boys waiting for him so that he could take each of them to a Boy Scout event, sports practices and games. Gene never complained but always did whatever was needed with the love that only a Dad who has passion for his children could do.

This passion for his children, however, was not sufficient to carry him through the whirlwind of his own emotions about other issues.

7

Come Into My Bedroom

I would like to invite you into the bedroom of my heart, where the darkest episodes of intense pain are felt. Often, the outward appearance is not an accurate reflection of the intimate emotions that play out in the privacy of one's heart. As I held on to the pillow of hope, soaking it with tears of helplessness and anger, I looked up and unrealistically expected to find Gene's strong hand to lift me up and offer the comfort I needed, only to find that the opposite was true.

Consumed with my own devastation, I neglected to devote the necessary time and effort toward what Gene might be experiencing emotionally. I couldn't look beyond the anxiety that my blindness had caused. Therefore, this anxiety affected negatively even the most basic aspects of the relationship between Gene and me. I was drained and had nothing left to give to him or anyone else.

He came home from work one evening and, with a cold and indifferent tone, not at all typical for him, informed me that we needed to take a ride. His demeanor was more silent than usual. I got ready quickly, putting on my bright red sweater and off-white corduroy pants. I don't know why, but the details of the clothing I wear in moments in which I face intense emotion are vividly engraved in the depths of my memory. I proceeded to comb my hair quickly and joined him as he silently walked me to the car. He opened the door; I slipped into the passenger's seat. Clueless about what he wanted to talk about, I clicked on my seat belt. He started the car and we rode silently as the car took us out of our neighborhood without any specific destination. Where we were going was not important because I wanted to know what was on his mind. I asked with curiosity and apprehension.

He began to talk to me with a tone of sadness and at the same time indifference. He informed me of his dissatisfaction with our marriage and our relationship. He explained that the lack of attention I had demonstrated toward him was painful. He added that there was someone at work he had been talking to about his emotions and had found comfort in her listening ear and her much needed understanding.

He continued talking, but the explanation and details that continued was a series of blurred but extremely painful lashes tearing at my heart. I don't remember everything he said. I wished I could have been numb; instead, everything, every feeling, intensified. That cold black bucket seat suddenly felt like an the electric chair, which was sending through me painful impulses of burning bolts, bringing me to a slow but agonizing emotional death. This blow coming from the one person I had relied on and never doubted poured over me like acid over an already burning body. It seared. I had already reached the end of my strength and energy attempting to cope with my blindness, but this rejection from Gene and his feeble attempt to make me understand why he had looked elsewhere for comfort and satisfaction was more than I could bear. I was stunned. I was speechless.

I wanted to escape, so I asked him to stop the car. I was becoming physically ill. He pulled in at a fast-food restaurant.

He walked me to the bathroom. Once inside, I felt my way through and reached one of the stalls. It seemed that I was emptying everything that was inside me, everything but the pain that was scorching my heart. For a moment, I imagined this small closed in area to be similar to the gas chambers used in the holocaust. Deep down I felt that this process to end a life might have been a merciful out for me because then I wouldn't need to face the reality of my broken world. But that wasn't going to happen. I had to step out and continue to face a darkness that not only covered my physical surroundings but my emotional one as well. I felt devastated and rejected. The weeks that followed became a series of blurry hazes, in which I felt that I was empty and hollow unable to sleep or eat.

I sensed that my world was hanging on by a thread as if I were dangling off a tall bridge. As I was desperately clinging on to the edge, my fingers were slowly slipping off inch by inch toward the edge as the weight of my body caused them to slowly lose their desperate grip. Rather than coming to my rescue as I expected, Gene had inadvertently stomped my fingers with all his strength, causing me to fall into an immense dark tunnel of despair.

In my view, I had no one else to blame. My blindness was destroying our plans and our marriage by shattering our dreams.

This was a fact. But it was also a fact that there were three little lives that needed at least one parent who was "together" enough to care for them. I needed to pick up the pieces somehow. But where would I begin? Should I try to cater to Gene's emotional needs? Do I fight and try to stay in a relationship, one that I felt that I had nothing to offer? Did I need to face the fact that the next step was to accept that I was soon to be a blind single mother?

Neither of us made a decision about the marriage. We sought counseling, but the advice was simply to "get out" of a relationship that wasn't working out. We talked, and talked some more, but nothing was resolved. Although Gene never said that he was leaving, our relationship certainly required healing. My blindness wasn't going away and his emotional needs were not being met by a wife who was unequipped to do so.

Once more, I tried to face what I saw as *my* problems alone. Through this desperate and dark episode, my instinct to "protect" those around me was prevalent. This included my parents; "I was just fine...don't worry," was my consistent response when Mom would ask how I was doing. Her deep concern and pain for me was easily heard in her voice as she offered to help me. They lived about ten minutes away from me at the time; this was probably better because they didn't have to witness the real pain all of us were going through. I wanted to keep her from really seeing my emotional devastation. She had enough to deal with because, at that very same time, my father also began to lose his sight. He was having serious car accidents. Fortunately, no one was ever hurt, but we all knew that he would soon have to come to terms with his ever-decreasing sight. Both of them had this painful and urgent decision to make.

It was the same with my friends, who were already aware of my diminishing eyesight. Those who lived near me did their best to help me by expressing their willingness to provide transportation for my sons and me. All of them were very much aware of my eyesight problem; so I decided to spare them the details of my marital problems.

In an attempt to put our life together again and move forward, I tried to seek ways to overcome this issue on my own. The thought of looking to God for answers was not foremost in my mind. Although I knew how to recite memorized prayers, God had not been a part of any plans I made, nor did I ever seek His input in this process. I had followed *my* dreams, *my* goals, *my* objectives...all according to the ever-present echo from the world to "follow your dreams." I was faithfully following this tempting and luring invitation. Never had I stopped to listen to God's calling or seek His direction.

If you had asked me if I believed in God, my answer would have been, "Of course, it's a personal and private matter, but I have him in my heart." What an answer! "In my heart?" God was out there somewhere, distant, abstract, put away in my mind, just there in case I would need to mutter a prayer to Him. Much like you put away your ATM card forgotten and disregarded, pulling it out only when needed.

I lacked a relationship with God. Therefore, when my dreams were broken, I felt lost, empty, and anxious. This anxiety drained me emotionally, making it more difficult for my adjustment to a life without sight. I felt rejected and abandoned by Gene and defeated by a force that was bigger than anything I had faced before. I found myself asking questions, wondering how could this have happened to me. I never wanted to alienate my husband. I never chose to be a blind person. I never wanted to be in the midst of a marriage that was falling apart. I never wanted to go through life in darkness. Since I knew what I did not want, I chose to dwell on what could be, a life with restored sight, and one that would eventually allow me to be the kind of wife Gene deserved. For this reason, I still held on to the hope that I would be able to see again, creating an intense and desperate desire to make that happen.

8

But Seek First the Kingdom

I decided to take action and seek aid from any and all sources. In an effort to be helpful, a friend told me of a psychic who would reveal to me where I could find a doctor who would cure me. The psychic, in reality, had no answers for me; instead she just left me more confused than before. Another friend suggested acupuncture. Those painful needles around my eyes were endured patiently week after week as I desperately hoped for positive results. A health and nutrition specialist offered her advice. Vitamin supplements became an important part of my diet. The goal was to strengthen my body and perhaps regain some sight back. This effort was also to no avail. I got to the point where I would have done any-thing...*anything* to be able to see again. I accepted a sugges-tion from a friend to seek the assistance of a "healer" who used crystals, smelling oils, and who informed me that she "felt the energy" around me. Who knows what else she did each time I visited her. She accomplished nothing except to lower the balance of my checking account.

Frustration and anger continued to dominate my emotions. I had been so successful in other areas of my life. Why was I unable to find something that could help me? I rationalized that if my sight would be restored, my marriage would be, too. But neither one was taking place. Therefore, my intense frustration gave me the urge to take the pieces of my life, enclose it neatly into a glass container, and throw it furiously with all my might against a wall!

So, what does one do when they reach this point of desperation? Pray! I prayed to God, the God whom I knew from my religious upbringing. I told him how unfair this was. I informed him that I didn't deserve this affliction. I pleaded and asked and continued to ask and plead. But in all my efforts to communicate with God, I never thought of stopping to listen to what He might have to say to me. Does God ever say anything to us? Of course not, those days were long gone. They belonged to ancient times where burning bushes spoke and miracles took place. But now we're in modern times, and biblical events are a thing of the past.

Now that I look back, I realize that I was terribly mistaken. I am convinced that God had something else planned for me because He put me in the very place where I had no option but to listen. This is how He brought it about.

The phone rang and I answered. "Hi, Jan!" called a friend whom I had not known for very long. "How are you doing!" she asked, concerned about what she knew I was going through.

"Just fine," I lied. The truth was that I was frustrated, hopeless, desperate, and defeated. I was everything but fine.

"Well, I didn't know how you felt but our church is having a service, which I think you might like," began her invitation.

Before I could give her my reply, she added, "There is a portion of this service where there are physical healings that take place."

My thought process changed immediately. "Really?" I asked with renewed interest. There was my answer! That is the miracle I was looking for! I would be certain to be one of those "lucky" people who would be cured instantly! "I'll go with you!" I replied with a sense of anticipation.

She picked me up that evening, and we attended the service together. The much-anticipated portion where the "healings" took place left me thoroughly disappointed! My eyes showed no change whatsoever! But I didn't give up. I thought, "Give it a few more chances." My rationalization at that time was that God would, much like a sweet elderly grandpa whom I never bothered to really know, be moved and grant me the miracle if I asked long enough.

With that incorrect perception and having no other alternative or any other source for hope, I continued to attend similar services. But there was a very significant difference. The subsequent services I attended did not make the "healing" aspect as their focus. They talked more about the Word of God. But even then, all I heard were teachings from the Bible with ambiguous concepts difficult for me to put into practice. It was difficult to concentrate because I was sidetracked by what my mind and heart held as the number one priority, to experience a miraculous healing. Therefore, with still some hope in the back of my mind, I continued to attend on a regular basis. These services were held in the evenings at a time when Gene could take care of our sons. The format of the sessions was similar to one another. It involved reading verses of the Bible, the leader's explanations, and shared discussions, as well as some touching testimonies by people who had gone through life-changing transformations.

Although I felt sporadic but fleeting feelings of comfort, I could not overcome the analytical view I always had when presented with something unfamiliar to me. The biblical concepts I had been listening to seemed to be a series of repetitious pulpit rhetoric. I knew that soon I would find a catch. I would learn that they had an ulterior motive for the seemingly comforting but irrelevant words they interjected as they addressed the crowd.

Chances are that everyone present at these sessions was burdened with some degree of personal problems, but I rationalized that none could be as bad as mine. I must confess that at times I had feelings that verged on the hysterical side of behavior. As I listened to all that was taught, shared and illustrated, I had the compelling urge to spring to my feet and shout, "Does anyone care about me? Does anyone know what I'm going through?" I wanted to scream at the top of my lungs, "You have no problems compared to what I'm facing! Do you know what it's like not to see a sunset anymore, or the stars at night, or the smile on your child's face!" Everything in me wanted to cry out, "Stop, stop your foolish singing! You can read the lyrics, but I can't. I can't do a lot of things anymore and have nothing, nothing to sing about!" Of course, my cries were not audible, but visible were the tears rolling down my face.

I felt resentment because, unlike me, all those ladies were sighted and were able to jump in their cars and carry on with their lives. They all could see and thus were more than capable to resolve whatever their issues were, they could see! But me, what chance did I have to move forward. I was living in a dark world, one which had no hope of any light coming through ever again.

My heart had become much like the metal folding chair I sat on, cold, hard, and lifeless. I hung my head down and shook it slowly, wishing, wishing for one more second. How I wished to see, just one more second, long enough to really see my surroundings just one more time. I wished to have that one second to really gaze at my sons' faces so as never to forget the images. One more second so that I could take one last look at life! But that second was not granted to me, not then, not ever.

How could they expect those Bible verses to have any relevance in my desperate situation? How would they be able to remove the bars that surrounded my dark prison? With my face buried in my hands, I sunk deep into my pain, into my sorrow, and into my hopelessness. I didn't want to look up; there was nothing to see.

What was even worse, my emotional state caused me to disregard or ignore one most important fact: the fact that although I could not see, God could. He could see beyond my desperate situation and had already prepared a plan for me. Of course, I didn't know this then, nor did I want to know. Perhaps I wasn't interested. What I wanted was my sight back, not God!

My heart was hardened, filled with resentment, anger, and anguish. So, just how powerful is this God of the Bible? Does He penetrate a hardened, angry, and bitter heart?

"The Lord does amazing things," echo the lyrics of a song. The Lord did begin to do just that with me...amazing things.

The first one took place when I stopped for a moment and allowed my heart to settle down enough to listen. Through my tears, I looked up and really listened enough to hear a tapping on my shoulder that was different, one that I had not known before. It came straight from God's Word. It said, "But seek first the kingdom of God, and His righteousness, and all these things shall be added unto you" (Matthew 6:33).

My world had reached the point where there was no place to go but up. It was as if God, through His Word in this particular verse, had gently held my chin, lifted it up, and whispered, "I have the answer." My heart heard that answer loud and clear...that He should be first in my search, not the restoring of my sight.

It was as if a veil had been removed from my eyes. Yes, I had been blind...really blind...from seeing His powerful hand. The priorities were clearly defined by Him, but it was me who had put them out of order. His truth had been right before my eyes, but I refused to see it. He had provided me the sight to recognize His sustaining power, but I had looked away. He put before me the comfort I needed but I chose to look inward and continue to cradle my pain.

"A choice, Jan." I thought. "You need to make a choice, whether to believe what God is saying to you or to dismiss it." Just because I might not believe it didn't mean that His Word was not true. I had been looking for tangible proof, the change in my heart was the undeniable proof, the clear evidence of what He says was and still is certainly true, real and relevant.

Eventually, the most incredible change began to take place. Bible verses were no longer ambiguous, irrelevant, or distant concepts. As my tears began to dry and my sobbing stopped, the clear calling from Jesus through His Word became the most effective spiritual white cane. It opened and cleared the path leading me toward the healing of my heart.

My spiritual vision had been restored through the Word of God. Yes, it was His most powerful word that was difficult to miss that provided me with the clear messages; they were directed right to me.

"What was the specific point when you knew that your life would take a turn?" asked a woman at one of my speaking engagements.

The verse that became the turning point for me was the one that gives the instruction to seek His kingdom first, above all. But how could I seek His Kingdom if I didn't even know Jesus Christ, the King! I knew all about Him, but really didn't *know* Him. Neither did I know how to begin this process. So I struggled.

The struggle stemmed from a life-long belief in the doctrines of my religion. I was convinced that it provided me with all I ever needed. Therefore, there was no reason for me to look or "seek" beyond on my own. I had an unshakeable faith – in my faith. Perhaps I had become bound to a religion and needed Christ to set me free!

9

Salvation

"I'm sorry…I won't be able to attend this Friday's girl's night out," I explained to one of my friends.

"Are you going to one of your 'churchy things'?" she responded with a hint of ridicule. I'm sure that other friends of mine also noticed that my focus had changed. It now clashed with the one I held before. Lunch with friends, shopping, and gatherings to work on "crafts" moved to a lower rank in my priorities. Although I still enjoyed their company, I reserved more time to what would, for me, bring a longer-lasting and complete satisfaction.

I found that when my heart was beginning to open to God, my outlook on life was also beginning to take a turn. I was changing. My perception of Bible verses was radically different than before. As I became familiar with them, they sparked a hunger to know even more. Rather than seeming insignificant and/or unimportant, the Word of God became my spiritual food. I looked for opportunities to learn. This included any Bible teachings, programs on TV or on radio that expanded on the knowledge of God.

I distinctly remember a program, which I previously

thought of as one that would be suited for those who "had no life." I thought it to be just too boring for me. But now what I was hearing drew me to really listen with more than just a simple interest. They talked about God in relevant ways. This was the very popular television show, *The 700 Club.* One day, while folding laundry, I was taking in the discussion topic between the host and his guest. I was drawn in by Sheila Walsh, more than just her Scottish accent; I was admiring the conviction with which she spoke referring to her faith in Jesus. At one point, they proceeded to extend an offer, an invitation to call a number, if anyone needed prayers. I called and the lady who answered patiently listened to my situation. She then proceeded to lead me in the sinner's prayer. This is where I accepted Jesus as my Savior. I repented of my sins and recognized that He died for them and expressing and believing in this truth, I obtained my salvation.

"Let me explain what salvation really means," began the lady with a most loving tone at the other end of the phone line. Initially, I was a little perplexed at the presumptuous notion on her part that I might not know what this concept meant.

"Doesn't everyone who believes in God know this?" I thought as I agreed to listen to her explanation.

The truth was that I didn't know...not really. My mind held learned doctrines, and I assumed I understood all there is to understand. Her explanation, however, was possibly more sobering and clear than I would have wanted it to be.

What was I really saved from? The answer was simple. I was saved from the wrath of God. He created hell for those who choose to reject Him. He gave us the opportunity to be saved and because His love is so intense, He gives this same opportunity over and over again. His desire is not for us to have eternal death. He created us to live forever in heaven with Him. When we make Christ the center of our lives, even physical death doesn't interrupt our relationship with Him.

It was precisely that relationship that I longed for with

every fiber of my being, not so much to avoid eternal death, but to satisfy the hunger for something solid and trustworthy. As I began my walk with Jesus, my perception on life changed dramatically. I no longer held on to anxiety or desperation because of my inability to see. The reason was because, although my physical eyes no longer performed their function, my hearing was more acute, and the listening ability of my heart was now tuned in to a different voice.

For the purpose of illustrating a point, I'd like to briefly fast forward my story to the time when Jason and Jeff were twenty-four and twenty-two years old respectively. Most moms will understand that no matter how old they get, it's nice just to hear our children's voices from time to time. I often called Jason because he was no longer living at home. He lived in an apartment close to the college he attended. I like to just "keep track" of him. Although Jeff still lived at home with us while he finished college, we hardly saw him because of his busy schedule. So, as a "pesky" Mom, I would call him on his cell. Often, I would find him in his car. "Hi, Jeff!" I would greet him.

"Oh, hi, Mom!" he would reply. Then I would begin to ask him some simple questions. I knew that he really didn't hear me, so I would repeat myself. "I'm sorry; Mom...let me turn the radio down."

"Good idea," I would think with relief. I could hear the blaring music in the background, and I was glad when he recognized that it gets in the way of us carrying on a conversation.

I had to do the very same thing spiritually. I had to turn down the volume of the world's voice, the loud blaring sound that repeats over and over that a blind person can't possibly live a life full of joy and abundance, the voice that echoes, "You're not complete if you lack a physical attribute." It convinces you that by being blind you're unable to fulfill your role as a wife. I made the decision not only to turn down the volume, but turn it completely off and disconnect the wires. This would guarantee that my ears would only pick up the straightforward, clear, and trust-worthy Word of God! I became deaf to the world's decep-tive lies. With full attention listening to my Savior, I was able to move confidently sightless into a sighted world.

My Surrender – Our Gain

God's voice was loud and clear—the battles I faced belonged to Him. I had been holding on to my struggles, turn-ing them into a burden that weighed a ton—it was time to turn them over to Him! Consequently, my decision, a very impor-tant one, to surrender the torment due to my physical and emotional darkness to almighty God is precisely what allowed him to begin the healing process. It was as if Jesus was silently scooping up the broken pieces of my heart, dust-ing them off and wiping away the hurt and the pain. He was then lovingly and gently placing each piece in its proper place. Once whole again, He then filled my heart with His kind of love, one that I accepted by placing Him at the center. This renewed heart had no room for self-pity, resentment, vengeance, or anger. The love it now held contained the abil-ity and willingness to forgive. This genuine forgiveness brought about freedom, and with it, the wisdom to make deci-sions logically and calmly. With serenity and confidence I gave Gene the freedom to stay or to leave. Whatever his deci-sion, I would win. If he chose to stay, Christ would take care of healing our marriage. If he left, Christ would also be the one who would fill the void of his absence.

Gene surprised me one evening when he came home and announced that he had put in his resignation. As a sign of his commitment to the family, he would seek other employ-ment. He was willing to start over with no distractions. I am convinced that God honored this decision on his part. He blessed us with another position for Gene in a company closer to our home.

I was extremely happy with this decision on his part. But I was still cautious…would this commitment be one that would last the life of our marriage? Rather than doubt or question his renewed commitment, I made the decision to focus on God, on his promise, on His Word, my gaze was fixed on Him and Him alone as my heart also repeated, "Thy Word is a lamp unto my feet, and a light unto my path" (Psalm 119:105).

There was no need to attempt to figure out what would happen in the distant future. A lamp can only provide enough lighting to see one step at a time. It was precisely God's Word that gave me the reassurance that He would provide me with the moment-to-moment guidance as well as the security necessary for each day.

Looking back at the series of events that took place, I can assure you that "I waited patiently for the LORD; and he inclined unto me, and heard my cry. He brought me up also out of a horrible pit, out of the miry clay, and set my feet upon a rock, and established my goings" (Psalm 40:1-2).

The Real Healing

As this verse points out, Jesus had in every sense brought me up also out of a horrible pit. Climbing slowly out of this dark and cold place, I began to walk with Him, warmed by the light of His Word. My heart began to fill with peace, a peace beyond what I could understand. The reason it was difficult to understand was because my walk with Jesus had nothing to do with an intellectual understanding. It had everything to do with a changed heart, one that allowed Jesus to reside in it and take control.

What is the purpose of a heart filled with Christ's peace? It becomes the eyeglasses, which give 20/20 vision in any situation. It was all clear to me now. I could see where we had been, what we had done, and where we had come. Gene and I had mistakenly relied on our own limited human wisdom and judgment, as well as that of secular counselors. In doing so, we had taken steps backwards, sideways, and in circles. Gene and I were both consumed by our own emotional impact due to my blindness. I was destroyed by the helplessness I felt. He was bewildered by his own lack of control of the situation. I felt cheated by him, by God, and by my world. He felt the unfairness of the whole thing and the need to seek answers on his own. We both looked for solutions on a horizontal line...overlooking the need to look vertically—to Almighty God!

Looking up with a mended heart, I knew who had healed the pain. I recognized exactly who had removed the anguish, one that had previously consumed me. As I looked to Jesus with gratitude, I also looked to Him for guidance. It was then when I was able to have the necessary confidence and wisdom to establish the boundaries for our marriage. God's wisdom gave me the words to express to Gene just exactly what was important to me. I was able to explain to him clearly that my first priority and my main focus was to serve and follow my Savior. Gene accepted this conviction.

I never made it a point to question or judge Gene's own walk with Christ, but one thing I knew with certainty—God was in control of that, too! Although I wasn't sure what Gene's reaction would be, I proceeded by asking him to respect my need to look to Jesus for everything, particularly our marriage. What I wanted most was to bring into our relationship the one crucial component. The most important one which would hold us together. Gene agreed. With Christ as this essential part of our marriage, it became the three-strand cord difficult to break. The chances for the success of our marriage multiplied.

We made diligent efforts to be more focused on the

priorities in our lives. God had put before us three responsibilities that had to hold a high priority. Our sons were and
continue to be a priceless gift from God. Sadly enough, we
had inadvertently disregarded this fact as we attempted to
resolve our own individual issues. I believe it was clear to
Gene, as it was for me, that we needed to cherish, treasure,
and value this gift even more than ever now. Gene agreed
to be led by the need to honor God by fulfilling our responsibilities as parents. We recognized the urgency to re-eval-
uate our purpose as a married couple before the eyes of
God. We made this commitment when we said our vows
before Him on our wedding day. Consequently, we could
trust that He would be the one to lead the way in this process. Yes, as He promised, He would take charge of our
lives. If we allow Him to do so, we could then put aside our
own selfish desires and follow him.

We took the first step, we began to pray together. It wasn't
easy at the beginning; actually, it was awkward and uncomfortable. The reason was because we had never done so as a
couple before and weren't quite sure how to begin. So we
started with the "Our Father." Eventually, and with simple
phrases, we began to talk to him as if He were there...He was.
I knew this for a fact because He honored this effort; He eased
our hearts and led the way.

The healing for our marriage had begun. The process to
move forward would be according to God's pace, not ours.
We had a job to do...trust in Him. In doing so, we could see
our relationship with different eyes, our situation with a new
attitude, and our love for each other with new value. More
importantly perhaps, it became evident for both of us that
what we desperately lacked was God as a crucial and indis-
pensable part of our marriage.

So, bottom line, what realistic effect did my "unhealed"
physical blindness play in our marriage? Looking back, my
inability to see initially became a crisis, one that without

Jesus would have meant the end for me and for our marriage. However, through Jesus, it became a useful tool. It was actually the channel through which we saw the need to refocus. In doing so, we could renew our relationship and reprioritize our values. We could also live up to our commitment to God and to one another. Most of all my blindness gave us the opportunity to see just how far God's faithfulness can reach ...I saw all this as a greater healing than the ability to see my surroundings.

10

Beginning My Career

Now, you're probably thinking, "...nice story with a happy ending." Well...not quite the ending, but the beginning of an incredible adventure. So, sit back and let me walk you through it.

The ones who benefited the most from the renewed commitment to our marriage were our three small sons. They now had parents with a much higher and important focus. We were able to move forward as a family. They also were all finally in school, and I had some free time for myself.

The thought of getting involved in something crossed my mind, but I had no idea what that might be. I still had little grasp of how to function fully with a visual impairment. Getting a part-time job didn't make much sense. We were blessed with Gene's income, which was sufficient. More importantly, I thought I would be very limited in the work I could do as a blind person. But God knew what I needed even if I didn't. Aware of my command of the Spanish language, a friend asked me to do an English translation of some material she had recorded in Spanish. She was so impressed with the results that she suggested that I consider serving as a Spanish interpreter.

My first reaction was to ask myself why would I want to work now that I was blind when I didn't work while I was sighted? In addition, although I had been to college, my degree in business administration had nothing to do with interpreting. Consequently, I had no exposure, preparation, or training as a Spanish interpreter.

"Are you sure you want to do this?" asked Gene when I informed him of this possible opportunity. "I'll support you all the way if that's what you want," he added with reassurance.

"You will have to take a test to assess your skills," the personnel assistant informed me when I called a worldwide interpreting company. I panicked for a moment. I had not taken a test of any kind since my years in college, much less in a field I had no familiarity with. Fear began to creep in, but God said, "Go forth."

I learned that often our minds are limited by looking only to human possibilities. In doing so, we miss the way God is able to make a way through impossibilities.

"A test?" I asked with a sense of renewed assurance, knowing that God would resolve what was before me.

"The test is oral?"

"Yes!" I thought. My hearing still works and so does my speech, thank you God, on with the test.

"If this is from you, help me Lord, do what I can't do for myself!" was my plea as I sat to take the test. He promptly answered that because my lack of sight helped to remove any visual distractions and my level of concentration was increased.

On the test, I rendered as best as I could what I heard in one language into the other. They must have been pleased with the results because when they called to tell me that I passed the test, they sent me to my first assignment at the Immigration and Naturalization Court.

This is when God, once again, was proving just how real and active He was in all areas of my life.

The court assignment was to be held in the courthouse in downtown St. Louis. Transportation and the logistics of my getting there were a concern. To resolve this, I called the Office of Blind Services for help. They suggested mobility training for me to navigate with the aid of a cane. But this wasn't an easy step for me to take because I had to first overcome emotional obstacles. Resigning to the fact that I had to get around with a cane seemed to me a humiliating experience! Me walk with a white cane? I would be just like one of those pitiful blind people that triggered in my mind thoughts of scorn. I wasn't ready to accept this degrading new image of myself.

I quickly realized, however, that this was the way the "old" me would analyze a situation. Now I had a different source, one, which fortunately corrected my unwise way of thinking. Bible verses began to come to mind and make perfect sense to me. Regarding my apprehension to be seen with a white cane, the Bible said this, "Pride goes before destruction, and a haughty spirit before a fall" (Proverbs 16:18). If I had chosen to give in to the feelings of vanity and pride, I would have brought about my own defeat. The manner in which I began to make choices now included God's input.

I called the agency for the blind and they were very accommodating. They promptly assigned me to a teacher. He was a gentleman with visual impairments as well who came in a cab to meet me. He introduced himself and handed me a white cane. He said it was compliments of the agency that sent him. He taught me how to move it from side to side to make sure that my path was clear. We then proceeded to get in the cab and head downtown. Once there, we got out and he began his teaching.

"The first thing is to learn how to use your hearing," he asserted. "Your ability to hear sounds will be the key for you to navigate through streets with traffic," he added with authority.

With the aid of the white cane, he taught me how to find steps, doors, elevators, etc. He also taught me how to avoid obstacles and how to get to my destination safely.

How very familiar all this was to me! I had gone through the very same instructions to learn to navigate through life. Who was my mobility teacher then? Jesus! In both instances, I learned quickly because I was put to the test on the very next day.

This time, it was in a totally unfamiliar place, a courtroom! That very word seemed intimidating to me. The only courtroom I had been exposed to was the one shown in the television program *Perry Mason!* Gene drove me to the building, which happened to be near his office. He walked me to the area where I would wait until my services were needed, and I could tell that he was somewhat concerned about leaving me there. He hesitantly said goodbye and headed to his office. There I was sitting nervously holding on to my white cane, wondering what I had gotten myself into! As I waited with visible fear and anxiety thinking of ways to get out of this predicament, I turned to the only person I could. I told God that if His promises were true, He would have to guide me through this experience that seemed impossible for me. His answer was, "For God has not given us a spirit of fear, but of power and of love and of a sound mind" (2 Timothy 1:7.)

"Are you the Spanish interpreter?" the court clerk asked as she came out to the waiting area. Everything in me wanted to answer with a resounding, "No," but I nodded shyly and proceeded to follow her voice, guided by my cane. I was helped to my seat and the session began. I was shaking with nervousness. Somehow I regained my composure enough to interpret everything I heard. All I did was pray for wisdom and proceeded to intensely concentrate on rendering an interpretation as accurately as I could.

After the session had gone on for a long while, actually it seemed like an eternity, the judge called for a recess, and he asked me to approach the bench. Guided by the bailiff, I obeyed, even more nervous than before. I was sure that he would ask me to go home and learn the skills of an interpreter before coming back. What he really said were the words that only God knew how much I needed to hear. He very kindly said that he was bilingual, and he had never heard a more professional and accurate interpretation before! He continued with other words of praise, which I cannot recall since I was in shock at his feedback. The attorney representing the United States was a Hispanic gentleman who also encouraged me. He said that the criminal court needed interpreters like me, and he kindly gave me the name of the person to contact.

My trust in God was not in vain, and His promises are true! I began an intense training program to develop my skills further. I was diligent in increasing my vocabulary and practicing simultaneous interpretation every moment my sons were in school. My mom and Gene looked up legal terminology for me to add to my vocabulary. Before long, I was rendering my services for the municipal, state, and federal courts in a variety of proceedings ranging from arraignments to murder trials. Soon, I began to receive letters from judges and attorneys who humbled me as they related their admiration and praises regarding the quality of my work.

God Provides

I was slowly learning that the goodness of God has no limits, and this was true in my work as well in all other areas of my life. While I always wanted to be there when our sons came home from school, transportation to and from the courtrooms was somewhat inconvenient and took time. Yet God made it easy for me to do this.

Not long after beginning my work for the courts, He put in my path a friend who informed me of a company, which was looking for interpreters who would work out of their homes. The interpretation was to be done over the phone, with no need to go anywhere. I applied for the position and was hired without any obstacles. Their main office was located in California, so the interview was done over the phone. There was no appropriate moment in which to inform them of my blindness. The work began almost immediately and once again I had to take the first necessary step by seeking God's guidance and wisdom to do the task well.

The courtroom interpretation is done simultaneously, but the phone interpretation is done all in the consecutive mode. This presented a problem for me because I needed other skills to perform this task. Unlike the simultaneous mode, where the speaker continues on without pausing for interpretation, the consecutive mode requires the interpreter to listen attentively, take quick but accurate notes, and, while the speaker pauses, render an immediate interpretation. Often the information is given in long segments and includes a variety of numbers and, at times, some difficult terminology. I needed divine intervention in order to be able to retain all the information given. Unable to take notes, I had to process what I retained in my memory in order to render the interpretation accurately and timely. I know it was God's doing because I was able to do so successfully. With each call I took, I made every effort to portray to each client extreme courtesy and respect with the hope for his or her patience in return.

God's blessings continued as two years later I was honored with the highest performance award presented by the company. Needless to say, this achievement thrilled me beyond words. They were kind enough to fly Gene and me to California and present it at their annual awards function. By this time, a few close colleagues knew about my visual impairment, but since I was to meet them all in person, I had no choice but to tell them about my complete blindness. I was told later that many were in awe as I was assisted to the front of the auditorium and received this award. I was never sure if this was because a blind person achieved this distinction or the testimony I gave of Christ in my life as I accepted it.

God continued to work in my life by providing all I needed to be successful. As the years went by, He directed me to new and easier ways to navigate without sight. I had no idea that technology had advanced to the point where a voice synthesizer could read a computer screen. Using key commands, one can navigate through material on the screen. Without the need to look at the monitor, you can work in different applications and "read" documents with the aid of a voice synthesizer. As it's to be expected from a loving God, He put in my path an agency that would provide this very tool for me. This allowed me to record and file information, create documents, send and receive e-mails, fill out forms, and do any work that a sighted person can do. This electronic assistant provided to me by the company I work for is no longer an electronic device, but part of my brain. I rely on it as I approach any assignment with confidence. I still need to learn quite a bit, but so far I'm able to function and perform as my sighted colleagues.

My main responsibility now is to interpret court proceedings, which are held in any number of various courtrooms in the country. But arriving at this point of my career was not simple. I had to also do a "first" regarding this milestone.

Because I can do my work anywhere in the country, my job with this company continued when our family moved to Florida in 1996. The move was good for all of us in a lot of ways, but I faced yet another obstacle: To obtain my state certification for the court system for the state of Florida, a rigorous test had to be taken. But giving such a test to a blind interpreter was an unprecedented process for them. Consequently, with the cooperation of the court system personnel, we were able to figure out just how to give me the written and the "sight translation" portions of the test.

I imagine that a test given in Braille would have been the best and easiest solution for all. The offer to learn Braille was made to me years ago, when I was still working for the court system in St. Louis. As I evaluated the possibility of learning this skill, I decided that it would not benefit me as I performed my duties as a court interpreter. The time it took to "write" words in Braille would diminish my ability to render the timely interpretation needed for court proceedings. My computer with a voice synthesizer replaced the need to learn Braille.

Although this skill would have come in handy at the time of the state exam, I made up my own ways to get over the hurdles that came my way regarding this test. The oral portions to test the consecutive and simultaneous skills were no problem. Other portions did provide a challenge. I had to request the assistance of a very kind court employee who would read me the questions on the multiple-choice test. But I had to figure out how to retain the various choices in my memory in order to choose the correct answer. As I listened carefully, I assigned the answers to my fingers. For example, my index finger was "A," the middle finger was "B," and the ring finger was "C" and so on. As soon as I heard an answer that could be a possible choice, I would hold out that finger while my hand was on my lap. This needed to be done very discreetly. Why? Because if the person happened to glance at my hand and the answer was "B" oops!

I passed all the portions of the test with a grade that surprised and pleased me immensely. I knew by now that working as a team with my Lord always brings results that go beyond expectations. This is when He gives me a spiritual "thumbs up."

Since I was the only blind person in the company, I had no clue what challenges I would have to overcome in order to maintain the same level of performance as my sighted colleagues. With the new technology at my fingertips, my work has expanded, and in the past several years, I have been blessed with opportunities to perform various functions for this large over-the-phone interpreting company. Of course, God continues to be behind all of this. He allowed me to perform each one of them successfully. He guided me as I glided through any tasks required for the position.

I am always delighted and flattered when my employer entrusts other new projects to me. For example, I thoroughly enjoy the facilitating of training sessions. They are obviously all done over the phone. The participants, who are located in other parts of the country, are not aware of my visual impairment. Although I'm glad to explain how I do things to anyone, I find that there is no need to share this information with the trainees.

But since I'm relating my story to you and not providing you any training, I will share with you just how this is done. One side of the headset I wear is connected to the computer. This allows me to key in various commands activating the voice synthesizer as I hear what it "reads" to me. With a speed and manner I choose, I am able to hear the contents of the files pertinent to the subject I'm teaching at the moment. I can also hear as it reads to me other files such as the attendance list. The other side of my headset, which includes a mouthpiece, is linked to the phone line. This allows me to simultaneously hear the participants as I interact with them, answering their questions or responding to their comments. But just in case you're thinking that this is a piece of cake since the computer does it all for me and my brain is elsewhere ...not so. I do put my brain to work from time to time. In order for me to address the participants by name and track their participation, I memorize all their names. Why? Because at times when I need to call them individually, it's easier and quicker to scroll down my memory rather than the screen. As a whole, I value this opportunity to practice this ability God has given me. For that reason, the positive feedback given by the participants at the end of each series of sessions might possibly hold more meaning for me than perhaps for any of my sighted colleagues.

God's abundant blessings beyond my expectations continue. In January of 2004, I was again extremely touched by receiving an unexpected award from my employer; one which honored and pleased me immensely. My heart was filled with gratitude as my dear colleagues graced me with a standing ovation as I accepted the highest recognition—the Professional Excellence award.

Timely Answers

Now that you have a glimpse at just how a blind person holding on to God's hand can successfully achieve anything in a sighted world; I would like to ask you a question. Would you agree that I've come a long way? By that I'm referring to the direction this career path of mine has taken. Do you remember back when I related to you my sheepishly feeble attempt to get through my first interpretation assignment? I was holding on to my white cane for security, but my heart cried to God for help and He responded. His Word said to me that He has not given us the spirit of fear, but of love, of power and sound mind.

Well, now you and I know exactly what He meant. Not the sound mind to operate a fancy computer and perform well at a job. Not at all! I believe He was referring to a sound mind to have the wisdom to trust in Him every step of the way!

My computer responds just exactly the way I expect. I key in commands and it very quickly responds with exactly what I need it to do. It is also the same with a faithful God, you trust in Him and He responds by opening doors. You lean on Him and He responds by strengthening you. You make a request in faith...aha! Here is the difference from my computer, God may not grant that request automatically. But with patience and perseverance on your part while you wait for His answer, He always grants them not only at the time best suited for you but also in ways that greatly exceed your expectations!

11

A Trip to the Mall

At times it seemed like Jesus transported me on a magic carpet from one life to another. From a life of resentment, ugliness, and darkness to a life of fullness, light, and joy.

I sure have come a long way from the time when I felt resentment for so many things. One of them was because I had lost my freedom to drive to the mall. Looking back, I feel a hint of embarrassment for the shallow way in which I set my priorities.

But now it's different. Not only are shopping trips a very low priority for me, there is no time! My forty- to forty-five-hour job from Monday to Friday keeps me busy during the day. Weekends are the time for the family. Evenings are full because I faithfully attend my ladies' Bible study as well as a couples' Bible study with Gene. I also work on a ministry in our neighborhood. And, of course, it's necessary for me to prepare to teach Sunday school in our church. I also enjoy thoroughly my weekly Toastmasters meetings. Gene and I like to spend time with friends, so making sure that we have the opportunity to socialize with them is important to me.

What do I do in my spare moments? I work on a variety of personal projects…you happen to be reading one of them!

I have always enjoyed spending fun moments with girl-friends. So if one of them would call and invite me to go to the mall, I usually accept because I know that we'll enjoy the time together. Unlike before, I don't accept because I have a need to visit the mall, but rather because it's an opportunity to enjoy her company and have a great time. Every time we go, I come home with stories to tell. Shopping with blind people is quite interesting and at times humorous. I have had sales clerks ask my friend questions such as, "Do you think she likes the blue or green sweater?" Why would they direct that question to my friend when I'm standing right next to her? Perhaps when my friend told the clerk that I couldn't see, she assumed the hearing is gone, too! Well…that doesn't happen all the time because there are other clerks who ask me a question by speaking very loudly and with a slow and clear tone. I wonder if they think I might be able to see a little if they spoke louder? I still love them and never miss an opportunity to express my appreciation for any help they provide.

There are also some embarrassing moments. Actually they are very embarrassing at the time they take place, but later on they become reasons for us to have a good laugh. One such instance was when a good friend left me standing by the checkout counter of a clothing store. "Wait for me here," she instructed while she went off to look for an item she knew I needed. I obeyed her orders and stood silently to the side of the counter. After a few moments, I heard the nice clerk say, "Can I help you?"

"Yes, I'm looking for a black skirt, size 6 petite," I said.

"Yes, ma'am," she responded politely.

"Do you know if you have that size in this department?"

"Yes, ma'am," was her answer.

"Would you please find it for me because I'm visually impaired?" I requested.

When her answer was, "I'll transfer you to that department," I realized that she had been talking on the phone and not to me!

Those shopping trips with my friends are, more than anything, an opportunity to have fun. I am very blessed because Gene has excellent taste in clothing, so as a rule he picks out the majority of my wardrobe. But Gene is not always there when I am getting dressed for the day or an event, so the question is how do I get dressed and coordinate my clothes, shoes, and jewelry. Well, as soon as I get a new garment, I feel the fabric, memorizing the color and any particular characteristics about it even before I hang it in my closet. By doing this, I can easily feel each item and know exactly what it is, the color, and what to wear with it. I do the same with shoes. Each shoe is unique in the heel shape and form so that all I have to do is remember the color. This way, I don't need to see them. Just feeling them tells me all I need to know. The pieces of jewelry I have are also very different from one another. I store all my silver in one place and the gold in another.

What does all of this have to do with my spiritual journey? Well, when you walk down the path of life with Jesus by your side, He guides you through a better route. Much like a tour guide, He doesn't leave you alone to walk through the traps of stress, tension, and anxiety. He instead, leads you to enjoy the abundance of the journey, one that includes laughter, fun, and enjoyment!

12

Teaching Them To Laugh

I know that a sense of humor is essential to maintain a healthy disposition, and I wanted my sons to learn this important lesson. I hoped that they would apply it as they were faced with negative situations. I have often laughed with my sons when they would try to "trick" me. Sometimes they would succeed and sometimes they wouldn't. For example, their favorite time to try to do this was at bedtime.

Making my rounds to all three of their rooms to talk and pray was a nightly routine. I was like most moms: No matter how often I tried to keep their rooms clean, the floor always seemed to be the "catch-all" for everything. As I walked through the door, I began an endless series of repetitive motion—bend over and pick up whatever met my feet, gathering any number of toys, shoes, articles of clothing, etc. With one arm full of these items, I would reach out with the other to find first the bed, then the pillow. But when I approached the bed of one of them, I noticed that he was more silent than usual. Thinking that he was sleep, I proceeded to bend down and gently kiss him. But rather than finding his chubby face, I found his feet wiggling on the pillow…he had gone head first under his covers!

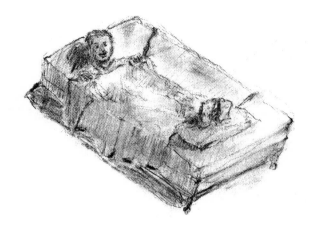

On another occasion, when Jeff and Joe were very young and we were still living in Missouri, they were playing in the backyard when I heard something hit the glass patio door. I opened it and stepped out onto some small rocks. They had been throwing directly at the glass door. I called them in and sternly began to scold them. But when one of them answered with a tone of disrespect, I proceeded to take him and sit him on the couch. While standing in front of him, I began to lecture and explain to him why his behavior was unacceptable. Proud of myself for the success I was having in bringing out his submissive silence and his seldom-seen quiet nature, I continued with my explanation and words of wisdom regarding the consequences of what he had done…only to find out that as soon as I brought him to the couch, he had quietly slipped out. I was lecturing to an empty couch!

When Joe was still young, he would tell his teacher about his mom being blind and convince her/him to invite me to his class to share with the students about the "mysteries" of blindness. With a mischievous tone, he later admitted that he did this not because he wanted his friends to learn something but because this was a way for him to have a break from schoolwork.

Looking back, I can now remember the times that being blind also had its advantages. At one point, our oldest son Jason decided that when he watched a movie on TV, the room had to be pitch black. His two younger brothers also followed that insistence. I had no problem with that; it certainly made no difference to me. My sight was the same with or without any light. Once, soon after a movie started, they asked if I would make them some sandwiches. I promptly complied and walked into the kitchen, which was adjacent to the TV room. As I began to get out the condiments and make the snack they had requested, they stopped and voiced their gladness and amazement at the fact that there wouldn't be too many moms who could prepare something to eat in complete darkness.

It was also at that time when the whole family began to jokingly call me the walking phone book. God's abundance had allowed my memory to develop to such an extent that I was able to commit to memory any amount of phone numbers. I imagine I stored them in my brain as a form of habit. But it was truly a blessing because it seemed that this information was always needed with urgency such as when they needed to call a friend at the last minute for a ride. Even to this day, our family doesn't own a written phone directory, there is no need—their reference is called "Mom."

Along with my memory, my ability to hear also sharpened. I could hear any sound, no matter how faint it may seem to others. This was not good news for our sons because whenever they tried to get away with something, my ears would pick up any plans being whispered by them or by any of their friends. This ability of mine was also to my advantage when it came to "watching" their intake of junk food at inappropriate moments of the day. The rule in our home was to limit drastically the soda and snacks lacking nutrition. This rule was broken only when we had company. In these instances, I imagine that the temptation was quite strong for each one of our small sons (or Gene) to devour the remaining goodies after company left. But when I was on guard, they had no chance to get away with it. I could hear the "swoosh" of a bottle of soda being opened from anywhere in our large home. The sound of a bag of potato chips had a distinct call to my ears, prompting me to check and put a stop to this kitchen invasion by little men.

Other Adjustments

They didn't stay little for very long. As they grew, each stage of the boy's lives brought about new and necessary adjustments for the family to cope with my blindness. Not all of them were simple. By the time Joe, Jeff, and Jason were in fourth, sixth, and ninth grades, my blindness was not a fact of life that could be overlooked anymore, and it created a more evident way for them to feel "different" from the rest of their friends. Each time they needed to go to school events or sport activities, they knew that if Dad was not available to drive them, unlike the other kids, their mom was not able to take her turn. As a result, they learned to swallow their pride and rely often on other parents, who would kindly pitch in and help. But I believe that what was more difficult for them was when they would have to inform their new friends that Mom couldn't see. I was never present when this information was shared, but I know that this particular age is often more sensitive of the image they portray; therefore, a mother who was blind certainly did not enhance this self-perception.

Fortunately, it didn't take long before our oldest son Jason turned sixteen. What a joy for him—and for me, too! He could now drive and provide rides for his brothers and me. As I was very much aware of Jason's excitement of having received his driver's license, I asked, "Okay Jason, how would you like to take Mom to a meeting at church?" Before I could finish the sentence he was eagerly accepting that invitation. I imagine that he welcomed any excuse to put to use that newly acquired privilege to drive. This stage is one of a great sense of freedom for sixteen year olds but also a source of great worry for the parents. I worried somewhat, but I was spared from the details that other parents actually see while riding with these novice drivers.

Don't think I got off easy, however. I still suffered some traumatic moments. The quick turns and close calls as my body would suddenly swing from side to side during the turns and the lashing forward when an abrupt stop took place gave me ways to pray I never knew before! On the other hand, I think that our sons were somewhat appreciative because they didn't have a mom who would sternly or in a nagging tone say, "Look out for that!" or "You're getting too close to the car in front of you." Having no other choice, I resigned myself to the fact that they would eventually mature and improve their driving abilities. I hoped.

13

Out of My Comfort Zone

❧

The house we lived in at the time I first experienced my total loss of sight was located in Affton, Missouri. It was an area near the neighborhood where I grew up, familiar to me and conveniently located. Gene and I had decided to build our home in a subdivision off one of the main but quiet streets. This was our first two-story, four-bedroom house, big enough for the five of us. I loved the design and everything about it.

The development was a brand new one and the houses were similar to one another. There were only four or five different models. The size of the houses varied from one story to two-story, some larger than others. They were lined up in perfect rows with the exact same size of carefully manicured lawns. The variety of shapes and sizes of perfectly trimmed bushes accented their landscaping. Some homes had colorful flowers to add to the contrast of the green grass. Since it was relatively new, the trees were not tall but were equally and strategically placed in front of the homes. The artistically arranged wreaths placed on some of the front doors added a touch of individuality. All these details put this attractive neighborhood in the category of a typical middle-class suburban residential area.

But the reason I loved this neighborhood wasn't so much because of the way it looked but because of what it meant to me. We had developed some very close friendships. The couples all around us were basically the same age as Gene and me. Their children were the same ages as ours and were also close friends to one another. We gathered for picnics, backyard barbecues, and spent time watching the activities of our offspring. We shared stories and supported each other in our challenges of parenthood.

All this was about to change. "The drive to work is draining me," Gene said one evening with concern in his voice. "I get home too late to take the boys to their activities," he continued to explain. Jason could not yet drive, and Gene held all of the driving responsibilities that couldn't be handled by our friends. "I really think that we should seriously consider moving closer to work," he said with determination.

I couldn't believe my ears. "What?" I thought with indignation. Deep down, I knew that what he was suggesting made sense, but moving so far away from the area that we knew so well would be difficult for all of us. Even if I were sighted the move would create changes that perhaps none of us were ready to make. But now that I was without sight, the thought frightened me. Starting all over again…all over again…new house to navigate in, new neighborhood, make new friends. I just couldn't do it, nor was I even willing to try. I realized that the one-hour drive for Gene each way was difficult for him, but going to a place where I felt unprotected and far from the familiarity I knew was an idea that I began to resent. The fact of going to an "unknown," since I was unable to see my surroundings, was terrifying to me. I trusted and felt secure in my familiar home, my neighborhood, and with my close friends.

Someone once said, "Lessons well learned come in

stages." I imagine that this period of time was one of those "stages" for me. The lesson to be learned was in the area of trust. When facing the unknown, trusting in God becomes not just a concept but a course of action. Looking beyond what "Jan" might feel or think I looked to Christ...to see what He would say. I actively sought to look ahead with anticipation to what He had in store for the family and me. I looked to see the next instruction He would give, "Every Word of God is pure: He is a shield unto them that put their trust in Him" (Proverbs 30:5).

God's shield is not limited to an area, a city, and a country or to any place on the planet. My refusal to move out of my comfort zone was a result of failing to draw from His Word. I knew it by heart but rather than to draw from it, I began to look for answers through my human reasoning. God's Word is always available, but failing to draw from it is like having a savings account with unlimited funds, but forgetting to make a withdrawal.

Our house went up for sale. The security of God's Word became the safe bridge that took us from one house to the other.

14

The Banquet Is Served

The house we moved to was located in St. Charles, just outside of St. Louis. We built it according to our specifications. Although far from our friends and family, I was pleased with it. It was large and comfortable; but what I liked best was that our neighbors became our great friends. Jason was fourteen, Jeff eleven, and Joe ten, and they adjusted to their new friends and schools better than I had anticipated.

This beautifully decorated house included a small but adequate office for me. I was grateful, since I had been working for my new employer for about a year, and my work was steady. The office gave me a private, quiet space to do the phone interpretations. It was on the second floor close to the master bedroom. I had my desk, my computer, a bookshelf, and a few other necessary pieces of furniture. The color theme was hunter green. The paint on the walls brought out one of the shades of color of the carefully placed border around the room. The perfect window dressing matched the colors in a large picture strategically placed on the wall in front of my desk. The silk flower arrangement on top of the bookshelf provided the last touch to bring together

the shades of green with the coordinating colors that surrounded my quaint office. How did I know all of this without being able to see? The answer is because I trusted in my
decorator's ability, knowledge, and wisdom. I had also put
my complete faith in God, whom I also could not see. I put
my trust in His wisdom as He arranged the events in my life
to blend them together and fulfill His divine purpose.

The work I did kept me in that office for eight hours
most days, except for periodic breaks. At an age when television is the main attraction in American homes, the radio
became for me the source not for entertainment but for education. I chose to listen to programs that would increase my
knowledge of the person of Jesus whom I had just begun to
know. My favorite station was one that broadcast Christian
programs featuring a variety of speakers. Chuck Swindoll,
Charles Stanley, John McArthur, James Dobson, and many
more. I really didn't know if they were preachers, teachers,
pastors or theologians. Their title didn't matter; what I found
fascinating is just how each would bring out a wide realm of
insights, ideas, advice, and revelations, each in his own
style. For example, Chuck Swindol's messages were easy to
understand and I found I could identify with whatever he
taught. He said at one point, that in any negative circumstance; 10% is what happens, but 90% is how you react to it.
I chose to adopt that perception as I faced life's setbacks. All
the speakers had one thing in common. They based their
sharing on the Word of God and their point of reference was
consistently the Bible.

Much like the constant and steady sprinkle of a hot
shower on a bitterly cold winter day, the sound waves coming from the radio reached my ears, soothing my heart with
the Word of God. The Bible references provided explanations and illustrations that helped me to reinforce and
expand my understanding of the Bible. The more I learned
the more I desired to know. Somehow I managed to find

opportunities in the evenings while the family watched TV to hear and study Bible precepts, ones that consistently seem to speak directly to me.

I was continuing to see just how my heart felt as I hungered for the Word of God. The satisfying of this craving was now filling my soul.

Perhaps I should to tell you that I have had a lot of experience in satisfying cravings. From time to time I have the opportunity to satisfy a craving for gourmet food. God is so kind and generous with Gene and me. He gave us the means to take vacations on a regular basis. Some we do as a family and some with friends. The absolute favorite vacation for us is taking cruises. We enjoy them so much that we go at least once a year. There is a lot to do, and I am selective about what I choose to participate in. Here are the choices: The islands are beautiful...so they say. The sun is warm...I already have olive skin, so tanning is not a priority. Shopping for straw items or souvenirs...not my thing. An occasional massage...maybe. A workout on the treadmill...for sure!

But when it comes to delighting in the exquisitely prepared meals...that is a different story. This is the part I really, really enjoy! All year long, I practice discipline in my eating habits. But when it comes to sitting at the tables in the elegant dining rooms inside those luxurious cruise ships, my mouth begins to water and my discipline goes out the window. I take my time and savor every morsel of delicious appetizers, salads, entrees, and no, I can't skip the rich desserts. As a matter of fact, I tend to spend the majority of the time enjoying each meal available to us. Gene's job is to patiently wait for me while I finish the last bite. I guess he must get tired of that because, on one occasion, he jokingly told me that he was thinking of just leaving me at that same spot, no need to escort me out of the dining room between meals. "Smart guy," I said with a sarcastic tone. But then I thought about it and said cheerfully, "Good idea!"

So I know first hand what it is like to completely fill one-self with something good. When I spend time on a daily basis savoring the delightful verses in the Word of God, I often find it difficult to walk away and go back into the world.

Similar to having the anticipation of sitting down for the meals on the cruise ships, I come before the banquet pre-pared by Jesus anticipating His comforting and reassuring words. They last through my day, providing me with nour-ishment and supplying me with spiritual stamina should I face any adverse moments.

I'd like to tell you what I have found to be the perfect diet of rich and abundant food for the soul provided in God's Word. It begins by saying that you will be blessed if you avoid certain traps or spiritual junk food—He has prepared some-thing much better for you. He follows it by saying what to do. He continues by stating what the results would be if you fol-low the courses of this spiritual banquet.

I reserved a place for you at this elegantly prepared din-ner table…the luxurious dining room is the book of Psalms. The menu reads chapter 1, verses 1-3.

Please take your seat…and let your heart enjoy!

Blessed is the man who walks not in the counsel of the ungodly, nor stands in the way of sinners, nor sits in the seat of the scornful; but his delight is in the law of the LORD, and in his law he meditates day and night. He shall be like a tree planted by the rivers of water, that brings forth its fruit in its season, whose leaf also shall not wither; and whatever he does shall prosper. (Psalm 1:1-3)

Allow me to share with you what this passage says to me. First of all, I often wondered why this particular psalm would be the very first one. As I studied the remaining verses, I realized that this particular message sets the tone and begins by providing the specific guidelines to follow in order to enjoy a successful life. Notice how God says that you will be "blessed" if you refrain from taking part in the activities mentioned at the beginning of the passage. I love this word because "blessed" is what you are as a result of God's grace shining upon you—it doesn't even compare to what the world might give you!

The passage continues by putting before you the various courses in a rich spiritual meal. It begins by stating clearly what not to do. But the main course defines just what to delight in and what to meditate on. (I also noticed that it required a meditation on a constant basis, not just once in a while!) The benefits are valuable. One would be like a tree planted by the rivers of water...there would be constant supply to stay vibrant and alive. The leaves would not wither...our spirit would not faint or dismay come what may. There would be fruit in due season...the results are guaranteed and they would be evident in a timely manner. Here is the dessert: Whatever one does shall prosper.

This is most definitely an affirmative statement from God's Word. There are no words such as "maybe," "perhaps," or "possibly." Rather, it is a *solid* promise. If one were to obey his instructions, He would allow prosperity to touch *all* areas of one's life. What is the clue word that indicates this? The word, "whatsoever"...meaning no matter what, of any kind at all, everything, no exceptions, it means all, yes A-L-L, ...*TODO* (in Spanish!)

Now you might know what God means when he says, "Oh taste and see that the LORD is good: blessed is the man who trusteth in him!" (Psalm 34:8).

15

The Correct Formula

Reading, studying, and applying Bible verses is truly a delight for me. But I also need to share with you that there are values and growth opportunities as well. At times, I am challenged by some verses. Some of them make me really think about the significance and its implications. What I mean is, that I wondered if God definitely meant to say exactly what the verse expresses? So, in order to make sure, I look for other verses that coincide and fully reiterate what He's saying. No matter how much I research...the message is the same! I am able to understand His Word even more clearly.

One such verse is in Revelation: "So then because thou art lukewarm, and neither cold nor hot, I will spew you out of my mouth" (Revelation 3:16).

What a graphic description of God's reaction to our lack of full commitment to Him! When I first read this verse it struck me. "Surely I don't fall in that category," I thought with relief. I was totally committed to God's Word; at least, I always tried to do my best. But when it came to push and shove, perhaps it wasn't so simple. There have been times in life when I, along with Gene, was very tempted to be "lukewarm" regarding our obedience to God.

In 1991 Gene was asked to join a small company as their controller. Without his knowledge, this company had already been in financial difficulties, and within nine months, the company was forced to go out of business. They left behind a number of sizable debts, including an extremely large one to the IRS. We were totally unaware of the penalty enforced by the federal government and that the officers and check signers are held personally responsible for this type of debt to the IRS. Gene and the two owners of the company were responsible for paying the $212,000 debt the company had incurred. This unexpected setback caught us off-guard and financially unprepared. Not knowing what else to do, Gene and I turned to God. It was becoming more natural for us to do so because we both were beginning to see more clearly His faithfulness in answering our prayers.

In a practical sense, we did not know how to respond to this unfair turn of events. It was draining all our savings, as well as forcing us to seek loans everywhere. It was necessary to take these measures in order to pay the extremely large amount. What made this impossible was the unreasonable terms mandated by the IRS. But the more we prayed, the stronger we felt the force of the IRS against us. The thousands of dollars spent in attorney fees and the constant battle to seek help to be released from this debt did not have any favorable results. It did not take long before we had nothing in our bank accounts. We had exhausted the borrowing options from banks and family members. Bankruptcy could have been an option but not an ethical solution. We still had our house and through the grace of God, Gene was able to find other employment. Yes, it was definitely the grace of God, a faithful God. We were in a difficult situation, but He remained just as trustworthy and faithful. Although the salary was garnished from this new job, we continued to have income. Unfortunately, the funds were spoken for and the debt hung over us like a dark cloud. The Bible says that we should "Trust in the LORD with all thine heart; and lean not on thy own understanding" (Proverbs 3:5).

It was difficult for us at times to follow God's instructions in this verse! He was telling us not to do precisely what we had been trying to do—figure out how this could have happened to us. We felt resentful for having been put in this undeserved and unfair position. Even though we never made sense of this circumstance, we chose to follow God's instructions and therefore not be overcome by anger, self-pity, and a vengeful spirit.

Although we were not overcome by any of these emotions, we did feel the stress and tension on a daily basis. What became my worst enemy was the mail. This was the way we constantly received bad news. At times, I found that other creditors seemed gentle and sensitive compared to the ruthless demands from the IRS. There was a period of time where we seldom saw a relief from those dreadful envelopes. Some were discouraging news from our attorney. He was brief with his negative update and clear with the request of his sizable fees.

Other pieces of mail would include a citation for Gene to appear in court. These appearances took place so that he could present evidence that would support his case proving his innocence...all to no avail. Some other letters were from the IRS. These dreaded pieces of paper would consistently bring unpleasant news. At times, they would inform Gene that he needed to meet with the new agent who took over the case. This was not good because the new agent was not familiar with the details and consequently, we had to start all over again. This delayed the process and consequently, would increase the attorney's time and input; thus proportionately increase his already large fees.

The evenings became the most dreaded part of the day for me. Rather than being a relaxing time at the end of the day, Gene and I would be forced to face and discuss the next step to take in order to survive this unwanted ordeal. I would wait nervously, dreading what he would read to me. The IRS rejected once again our plea for more reasonable payment plans. This government entity was to me a merciless tyrant. It was holding us prisoners behind imaginary bars of relentless force.

They were meticulous about making sure that they had access to all our funds. They included the income tax refund, which was seized to add to the payments. It seemed as if all our personal finances were property of the government. We no longer had any say regarding the handling of our funds. Everything had to be accounted for, from the dry-cleaning bills to the tuition we paid for our sons; it was all information that had to be scrutinized by the IRS agent assigned to us at that time.

I am so grateful that Gene is a man of integrity and faith. This commitment on his part was what kept him in obedience to God. My faith in Christ as I leaned on His Word was the only thing that kept me going.

We just persevered in prayer. We held hands, and, in our bedroom after the boys were asleep, we asked God to guide us and give us strength.

We were forced to set priorities regarding the spending of our money. Some things needed to be cut. We discussed cutting the regular tithing to our church. We knew that God would understand and help us anyway. We felt justified in doing so because, after all, this entire situation was out of our control, and we needed every bit of money to meet our family's expenses.

At this point, we weren't sure which way to go regarding tithing. Deep down, there were some verses in the Bible, such as the one about being "lukewarm," which we wanted to disagree with. But in doing so, we would have fallen into the non-committed category. This was undoubtedly a true test for us. We would see if we were really committed to God's Word or not. We were tempted to give in to the urge of picking and choosing those biblical verses that suited us.

Testing God

Malachi 3:10 says, "'Bring the whole tithe into the storehouse, that there may be food in my house. Test me in this,' says the LORD Almighty, 'and see if I will not throw open the floodgates of heaven and pour out so much blessing that you will not have room enough for it.'"

Who are we to test Almighty God? But this is precisely what He says in this verse, to test Him. The answer was clear. He promises to be faithful by blessing us abundantly. The Bible also instructs that we should give God the first fruits of our labor. It didn't say to do this only if we could afford it. The choice was simple, either we believed in God's Word and chose to trust in Him or we didn't.

Rather than discontinue our tithing, we faithfully continued to give back to the Lord week after week. We chose to do just as He instructed. But He remained silent during this time in spite of our constant prayers regarding our situation. On the contrary, things were getting worse because in addition to this ordeal, Gene's new employer began to lose business and would soon file chapter 11. Now we were facing not only a debt that was overwhelming to us but he was about to face unemployment as well. Discouraged by our unanswered prayers, we were tempted to question this faith issue, but we chose to persevere.

This became our formula: Prayer and perseverance equal exceeded expectations. God fulfilled His promise to the letter. We did our portion, pray and persevere. God was about to do his portion, exceeding our expectations.

Eventually, He led Gene to a diligent headhunter, who,

in a very short time, presented Gene with several employment options. Gene chose two of them to interview. One of them seemed very attractive, but since the candidates came from all parts of the country, the competition was intense. After the initial steps and interviews were taken, we waited for the response. Finally we received a phone call. Gene did not get the position he applied for. Instead they had reviewed his credentials, professional accomplishments, and experience, and this had prompted them to offer him an even higher executive position, which came with increased benefits, advancement potential, and a salary level that exceeded any of our expectations.

In a matter of one year, the debt to the IRS reached a settlement and we were able to pay it off completely. All the sizable attorney's fees, including the outstanding loans, were also completely paid off with interest. This is when God's faithfulness to our obedience was clear. Our savings began to accumulate quickly and more abundantly than it had in our twenty years of marriage.

16

He Points the Way

Florida was our destination as Gene began his employ-
ment with this new company. Moving to the Sunshine
State turned out to be in many ways a pleasant and warm
experience for all of us. Gene's prospective employer flew
the family to Orlando for the weekend. Our sons enjoyed the
theme parks, so this mini-vacation was an unexpected dream
come true for them. Gene and I, on the other hand, were busy
with a less-than-pleasant task of finding a house in a very
short time. We wanted to take advantage of the few days
available to us to find the right home for our family.

The very competent and friendly real estate agent
assigned to us by Gene's employer was very helpful. I liked
her right from the beginning.

"I'm so sorry Jan...I did it again!" she apologized after
the umpteenth time she asked me as she pointed out various
features of the houses we looked at.

"Jan, if you look over here..." or "Can you see over
there...?" Her apology for asking these questions wasn't
necessary. Everyone forgets my lack of sight and asks those
questions at one time or another; I had become accustomed.

"Can I ask you a personal question?" I said to her the minute I met her.

"Sure!" she answered with a warm tone in her voice.

"Are you a Christian?" I boldly asked her. Now, you must understand that there are many advantages to the inability to see: You can't see people roll their eyes as an expression of disgust, nor can you "see" gestures of annoyance or disbelief. As a result, I have become somewhat bold in what I say to people. I just assume they're smiling and have a pleasant look as they hear what I have to say.

Her answer was, "Yes, I am. Why do you ask?"

I had a very good reason for wanting to know this bit of information. I was going to seek her assistance to put me in touch with Christian friends. I also wanted to learn of any public schools that had Christian ministries working with the students. She quickly offered to give me a phone number of a Christian couple who worked with Campus Crusade for Christ. I had heard wonderful things about this organization and was excited to meet anyone associated with them. I knew that they offered ministries geared for young people on the college and high school campuses. I was so grateful to learn this because my sons would have the opportunity to be exposed to biblical teachings with activities designed specifically for their age group. Having that valuable information about Christian ministries, I was more comfortable about moving forward in the house-hunting process.

There was no time to build a house in Orlando. We did not want to move twice. There were now seven of us: Gene and I, our three sons, and my parents. Six years after I lost my sight, my parents came to live with us. This arrangement was truly a blessing for us. We all contributed to the household tasks according to our abilities.

Although my father had also lost his sight completely, he has a variety of activities he enjoys. He learned to operate his computer with the aid of a voice synthesizer similar to mine. When he is not sending e-mail messages to his brothers in Bolivia, he is visiting websites where he is able to read every section of various daily newspapers from La Paz, Bolivia, as well as other South American countries. He began this activity at seventy-five and could possibly be the most informed person in the world when it comes to current events in that part of the globe. He also finds tasks that only he has the time to do. These include taking care of the pool and the citrus trees. He gets around the house with the aid of his trusted white cane. He designed and, with some help from our son Jeff, installed an irrigation system for "his" trees in the back of our house.

My mom is tiny, but she's in constant fast-moving action throughout the house. She swiftly goes from one chore to another. She takes care of the cooking, the laundry, grocery shopping, and endless other chores. What we all admire most is the way she consistently radiates joy, tenderness, patience, and dedication to the whole family. Although Gene, with his incredible patience, has through the years read dozens of books to me, my mom has been my "secretary." She patiently reads pertinent information to me on a daily basis. She keeps track of the important and large amount of mail from my employer and other ministries I am involved in.

I enjoy taking care of the household chores, including all the cooking and trying new recipes, when my parents take extended vacations back home to Bolivia, but I'm always glad when they come back.

My parent's discretion in making sure that we have our time alone, as well as Gene's patience and acceptance, makes our home a place of peace with no conflicts of any kind.

This was the boisterous family looking for a new home in Orlando. Our home in St. Charles was built with a small but comfortable apartment ideally located in the back for my mom and dad. As we looked for a house in Orlando, it was important that we find a large enough home for all of us. As we began the process of searching for just the right one, we had to take the time for the verbal description I needed of each feature of the homes we saw.

Gene deserves a medal for his patience. The tireless manner in which he described each detail of every home had to be a tedious and annoying task. He never complained, but I sure felt like complaining.

After "looking" at countless homes, I felt dizzy trying to picture the layout and the size, design, and location of the rooms of one house after another. After a while, they all blended together in my mind. What became our source of reassurance was the fact that we knew that God would lead us to the right house. As soon as we got in the car and before we drove away to meet the real estate agent, we asked God to help us find the house he had in store for us. We were certain that he would lead us in our search. We didn't know just how He would do it because we were asking for something that seemed almost impossible. We had three days to find a house in our price range, with in-laws quarters, located in a nice area of Orlando and close to Gene's work. Quarters for in-laws are not a common feature in most homes, so the choices, as well as the time we had to find it, were very limited.

We finally came to a house that was not quite finished. We were running out of time and had visited just about all the homes that met our criteria in the area. We decided to purchase it, with the intention of adding the necessary rooms needed for the seven of us. Spending these funds for the addition was not the ideal scenario. I felt apprehension and uncertainty, but it seemed to be the only and last choice. We talked at length with the builders and agreed on the details. We were about to sign the papers and as we took the pen to do so, the agent abruptly stopped us. God might have used her at this point to show us which way to direct our path just as He promised to do for those who seek His help: "And thine ears shall hear a word behind thee, saying, This is the way, walk ye in it, when ye turn to the right hand, and when ye turn to the left" (Isaiah 30:21).

With an excited tone, the agent informed us that she noticed a house that must have just come on the market. The list indicated specifically that it had in-laws quarters. We went to look at it, and it included everything that we needed. It was the perfect house, right location, adequate size, and within our price range. Looking back we realized how close we came to making a decision that would have been the wrong house for us. As expected, God answered our prayers by guiding us to the right one!

We signed the papers that same afternoon. All the steps necessary for the transaction were accomplished on that same day—as if God was orchestrating all the steps...He was! Gene moved within two weeks. Three months later we sold the house in St. Louis and the rest of the family joined him.

Memorization Is the Key

Once in Orlando, I began my usual method of adjustment. The process of learning something new required me to apply every ounce of knowledge, creativity, patience, and wisdom I had. Learning to live in a new house, neighborhood, city, and state presented challenges that with time I had no choice but to overcome. I used my own methods that worked for me and brought about practical results.

The first task at hand was to unpack the endless number of boxes that the movers began to pile up all around this big house. Fortunately, they were clearly marked and were placed in the correct rooms. Unpacking the boxes in each room was not difficult but it was very arduous work. I had only taken one week off work, and I needed to get the job done within that period of time. In addition, it was particularly urgent to clear the boxes from the house as soon as we could in order for me to begin to navigate throughout it.

Boxes all over presented a dangerous trap for me. With help from the whole family we completed the job in one week.

The decorating of our home was another task that was accomplished without much effort. When I went back to St. Louis, I took with me all the window measurements, color theme, and other details of the new house. By the time we moved into our new home in Orlando I had all the window treatments, wall decorations, silk flower arrangements ready to be put in place. Whereas I used a decorator in St. Charles, for the new Orlando home, I prepared all the decorations by having them made with the colors of the new house. My mom and I shopped for some additional ones, and we chose the appropriate place for each piece. It was important for me to finish this process quickly so that I could put it aside. I was then free to concentrate on more important aspects of our life in this new city.

Now settled in our new home, the next step was to learn to move around it without assistance. This task didn't take too long because I used the same method as I used in our previous home, judging the distance between the furniture and the size of the rooms by the amount of steps needed to get around them. Soon I was able to move from room to room with more confidence.

The first tasks had been accomplished. I was familiar with the house. Now I needed to learn the neighborhood and the streets in the Orlando area. My first step was to learn the names of the streets and their direction, north, south, east, or west. This was easily done as I asked Gene or my mom to let me know each name as we drove through them. I began to memorize them a few at a time. After a number of weeks, I knew exactly where the streets were, their sequence, the direction they ran, as well as the key landmarks along each one of them. This was important to know because if I needed to have someone drive me somewhere, I would be able to guide him or her with ease. The strange thing about all of this is that Gene relies on my sense of direction each time we go to an unfamiliar place. I am the one who gets the directions by memorizing them. I can then direct him by telling where to make the turns. I remember a time when we had a friend from St. Louis visiting us and he called us saying he was lost. Talking to me through his cell phone, he followed my instructions as I guided him through the city to our house. It was a simple task, because all he needed to tell me was the landmarks and names of the streets. As he did so, it was simple for me to determine what direction he was heading in order to guide him. There isn't anything great about a blind person's ability to navigate in an unfamiliar place. All it took from me was the willingness to learn, to memorize the information, and to put it into practice.

I took these same steps to learn scripture. I desired with all my heart to know God's Word in order to navigate through life. I memorized Bible verses. More importantly I learned to obey them by putting what I learned into practice.

17

Their Spiritual Walk

Once in Orlando, Jason enrolled in the local community college, and Joe and Jeff went off to middle school and high school respectively. Moving had been a difficult adjustment for all of them, particularly for Jeff and Joe. They came from schools one-eighth the size of the ones they were attending. The setting, format of classes, ethnic diversity, and rules were as different as night and day from what they knew back in St. Louis. I was glad when they chose to participate in sports. This helped to ease their adjustment into this new school culture. I knew that they would be okay. Deep down I felt that if I was able to survive a similar transition from one country to another, they could make the transition from one state to another.

Whether the boys were in private or public schools, Gene and I were always concerned for their safety, although I was more concerned with their spiritual protection and success, rather than their academic success. I wanted them to know, just as I did, the freedom of living a life in Christ. I had no doubt that God would answer my prayers. And while my sons' salvation was the greatest desire of my heart,

I knew that God would bring this to pass in His timing and not mine. I waited patiently and held on to this promise, "If ye abide in me, and my words abide in you, ye shall ask what ye will, and it shall be done unto you" (John 15:7).

My boys were also very much aware of my determination to encourage them in other areas that I believed were important, especially their nutrition.

"What's up with the whole-wheat pancakes!" complained Joe. "Why don't you make regular pancakes or chocolate chip cookies like other moms?" Joe was always more outspoken than his older brothers. Joe was right. I was not the kind of mom, who except for rare occasions, baked cookies or bought my sons treats. I would rather make every effort to teach them principles of good nutrition and self-control. I wanted to teach them not to give in to temptation in areas of less importance, so that they would know how to exercise self-control in crucial areas of their lives, such as resisting temptation to walk away from God.

I also was the kind of Mom who didn't push them to play sports. In fact, when Jeff and Joe were playing football, I told them that all I do is pray they don't get hurt. On the way home from one of the football games, Jeff told me to stop praying because he ended up sitting on the bench for a good part of that game!

They both excelled in every sport they participated in, just as Jason excelled in his artistic abilities. Even though I didn't push our sons, I did make every effort possible to encourage them emphatically to reach success in their spiritual life. For this reason the next step for me to take was to concentrate on plugging the boys into the right Christian group. We didn't succeed in our efforts to have them attend and participate in our parish youth groups in St. Louis, and this wasn't any different in Orlando. No matter how hard we tried or what we did to convince them, they found no interest in going. They attended a few times but only in obedience to Gene and me.

The results were different when I initiated a call to a youth leader of the Christian ministry called Student Venture. I spoke with a godly young man named Brad, who was assigned to the middle school and high school where Jeff and Joe were attending. I explained our situation. He expressed enthusiasm and offered to come to the house to meet the boys. I was so impressed with his willingness to take the time to get acquainted with my sons.

Brad set an incredible example for our sons. They immediately bonded with him, and he invited them to play basketball with him, as well as attend some Bible studies and meetings for Christian students. I could tell that they liked his company. I remember Joe telling me after a few weeks that Brad was his best friend.

It was this Student Venture ministry that God used for Jeff and Joe to begin their walk with the Lord. They weren't perfect boys; in fact, I would say that they were a real challenge for Brad, especially Joe. But Brad never gave up on them, displaying patience and commitment with them, as he did with all the youth he led.

The Brick

"All right I'll go..." Joe said, with little enthusiasm. This was in response to my emphatic encouragement to attend a Fellowship of Christian Athletes Summer camp. It was to be held in Black Mountain, North Carolina, during the month of July 1999. Typical of Joe's personality, he had always been ready to make the best of everything and enjoy whatever he was doing to the fullest. I am sure that he did his best to enjoy his activities at camp as well. At times, he included some mischievous behavior as part of this "enjoyment." One of these was not totally pleasing to the camp staff.

The biblically based series of programs, lectures, and explanations were prepared and creatively presented to the youth in ways that were relevant to their age. The most crucial concept was, of course, the explanation of eternal life through salvation. The invitation was made to come forward and accept Jesus in their hearts.

Joe was always the type of young man who would never do anything he didn't want to do. He was an excellent athlete even breaking records in football for his high school. He was strong willed—a challenge for me—but he had always been a very vivacious child, full of energy, charm, and wit. I think that a clump of white hair appeared on my head the minute he took his first step. However, God knew what He was doing when He created him. He gave Joe the qualities and personality of a leader. His friends and teammates respected him and seemed to follow his lead in many areas.

When it came to going forward and receiving Jesus, Joe led the group. He made a public commitment to give his life to Christ. He followed the steps by repenting of his sins and accepting Jesus in his heart as his personal Savior.

Joe was a leader, but nothing pleased me more than when he displayed signs of following Jesus. He came home from that camp noticeably changed. Then, with excitement in his voice he began to relate the following experience. The camp members had attended a presentation creatively illustrating the concept that building a house with bricks meant that it would be sturdy, strong, and able to withstand storms of any kind. Conversely, building your house with sticks meant that it would be flimsy, weak, and easily destroyed. The analogy was directed to the comparison to a life solidly grounded in Christ and able to face the storms in life rather than one without Him, vulnerable to adversity and destruction.

After this talk, Joe challenged five of the boys to do something crazy. While they stood at the foot of a tall mountain, they were met by Joe's typical and persuasive invitation. "Do you want to do something crazy? Do you want to climb a mountain?" Most of them expressed apprehension, but they admitted it was difficult to say "No" to Joe. Perhaps this invitation would have been better received by the sixteen and seventeen year olds had it not been for the rattlesnake warning, which had been officially announced that morning for those in that immediate area. As they hesitantly followed Joe, they came across a large dead black snake; they all stopped in their tracks not knowing what to do. Joe bent down picked up the snake, tossed it to the side, and said with determination, "Come on, let's climb."

The long two and half-hour climb was not easy. They grew tired, weak, and hungry. Some wanted to go back. Joe would dismiss their wishes by encouraging them to continue. As they got closer and closer to the top, the view and splendor of the clouds brushing against the trees gave them renewed energy to keep going. Any attempts of giving up were answered by Joe saying with insistence, "We made it this far, we've got to finish."

The final goal to reach the top was met by these boys

whose feeling of exhilarating joy served to take away any fatigue felt just moments before. They spotted a single, solitary brick lying at the very top of the mountain. In overwhelming amazement, Joe turned to the group and shouted, "Here it is, this is exactly what we were talking about!" Joe knew that this finding was neither coincidence nor an accident. He knew in his heart that God had put it there to bring them a more vivid message of what He intended their lives to be.

Each boy in the group understood the meaning. The message they had heard a couple of hours earlier in the chapel was made real to them in a way that would impact their lives in a powerful way. They formed a circle, held hands, and prayed, "Father, I thank you for this opportunity that we have to be up on this mountain close to you. I thank you for letting us find this brick because we know it's a message from you."

After pictures were taken of each other with the background of a breathtaking view, the group began their descent down the mountain. This time, however, with hearts of gratitude of a changed life, they carried the brick as a symbol of the message clearly sent to them by God.

Their excitement soon turned to concern because they realized they had not informed anyone of their trip up the mountain. This hike had caused a lot of worry for the camp staff because they had been unaware of the boys' whereabouts. They had been looking for them for hours. Although they might have deserved some kind of punishment, the coaches, the youth leaders and the staff in general were all amazed at the boys' story.

The brick has been placed in a glass case in the athletic department at Cypress Creek High School where Joe graduated in 2001.

18

New Friends

"Are you guys having company again? Didn't you have a family stay with you last week?" asked a new friend with disbelief.

It was true. Once in Orlando, we had family and friends from everywhere come and visit us. We weren't really sure whether it was that they wanted to see us, or the fact that we now lived in the tourist capital of the world. Whatever, the reason, I was delighted every time we had visitors who chose to stay with us.

Although we settled in and established a routine for all of us, there was something missing for me. "Was I really missing our home back in St. Louis? I can't be homesick!" I tried to reason with myself. "I'm a mature Christian now. I should know better, this is where God wants me to be and I should be grateful!" I attempted to rationalize.

The truth was that the routine I developed was missing one very important aspect of my life, a group of friends like I had in St. Louis. While living there, I had helped start a Moms-In-Touch group. The main focus was to gather on a regular basis and, by following God's Word, pray for our children. I thoroughly enjoyed the time spent with these dear ladies because I could see that God was working in our lives. Prayers were answered as we supported each other in our challenges of motherhood.

I sure missed that fellowship in a new city where I knew no one. I tried hosting one on my own, but because of schedule conflicts among the participants, it didn't last too long.

"Listen to this!" Gene announced with excitement. "They're offering a session for moms at the local church. You might like that," he suggested.

I was thrilled. I had visions of an opportunity to enhance and grow in my spiritual life. But I was thoroughly disappointed. The focus was on the "me" concept. The ideas presented centered on the need to look within us, nurture our needs, and cater to our own wants first. This was contradictory to what God expects. There was a point in my life when I focused on me first rather than on God. I certainly did not want to go back to that stage where the rewards were empty and deceiving. As they say, "Been there...done that!"

I kept searching and soon I learned of a neighborhood Bible study group that met in the evenings. What an interesting group! Unlike in St. Louis, where we all had pretty much the same background and shared so many things in common, these ladies were unique and interestingly different from one another and from me. They were a mixture of backgrounds, ages, ethnic descents, and faith denominations. Although I enjoyed our study sessions, the group was not stable. As is typical of residents of Orlando, who often don't stay in one place for very long, these ladies moved to different areas. With only four of us to continue, we made efforts to reach out to other women. Since we were not successful, we prayed for guidance, and God led us to a larger Bible study group in a nearby Christian church.

First Encounter

There are several situations, which can be a little tricky for a blind person. At times, when I meet someone for the first time, and if it's a casual setting, a simple, "Nice to meet you," as I look toward the place where his/her voice came from is sufficient. However, when the setting is a little more formal, I need to be more attentive. There was a period of time when Gene held an executive position for a large company. One of the benefits I enjoyed was the fact that we had the opportunity to attend elegant and somewhat extravagant events.

I looked forward to them because I enjoy getting dressed up and wearing fancy dresses. Of course the delicacies often served with the utmost care added to my enjoyment of such events. The only negative thing about such events was that I really couldn't relax like I would have wanted to. It was important that I be on my toes as Gene introduced me to his boss, his colleagues, and other important people in his company. I needed to be alert to feel his gentle but quick nudge to my arm, discreetly given, as someone would extend his/her hand when I was being introduced. Gene and I have always been up front with anyone when the time came to inform him or her about my lack of sight. However, these explanations to everyone at the moment of meeting him or her might have been inappropriate. So, with a cocktail in one hand, a smile on my face, I was free to shake anyone's hand...did I say a cocktail? Let me explain. One of my favorite juices is cranberry juice. I don't like ice in the juices nor in the water I drink. I ask Gene to get me a glass of cranberry juice with no ice. As I enjoy my favorite juice...it appears as if I'm drinking red wine. They might think I'm being a lush as I request a second drink!

When my friend and I walked into the group of ladies at the Christian Church, the setting was obviously quite different. But I still had to go through the first meeting process. By the time we got there, several ladies had already arrived. I guess the quickest and easiest way to introduce myself would have been to get it over with and simply say in a friendly tone, "Hi, everyone, I'm blind, it's nice to meet all of you!" No, that would not work. I would give them that information when the appropriate time came.

My friend carefully walked me toward a chair, she stopped, and I felt it as my leg touched it and proceeded to sit down. She sat next to me. I'm sure there were a variety of silent reactions from those ladies who observed me walk through the room holding on to my friend's arm. Later on, they informed me that they had no idea that I was blind.

What were those ladies like? Well…I couldn't tell you if they were older or younger, thin or heavy, tall or short, well dressed or frumpy, stylish or not. Actually, I'm glad that I can't tell you that. Why? Because if I could, it would be the reflection of the shortsightedness I had when I could see. The shortsightedness was linked to my attitude. Initially, I couldn't see past their physical appearance. I tended to judge people for their looks. My initial thoughts might have been "Why would she wear those pants with that top…they don't even match!" Or "Love that haircut. Wish I could get my hair to do that." Or I would silently criticize, "Doesn't she know the 'gypsy' look is out…all that jewelry…she could lose a few pounds, too!" I also confess that I have at times asked myself, "Wonder where she gets the money to afford that designer purse?"

But now I had the true blessing of being able to go beyond all that shallow and superficial view of people I encountered. It was then, and still is now, an absolute gift of having those distractions removed, allowing me to see people for who they really are. I loved these ladies because I could hear the tenderness in their voices as they greeted us with "Hello!" and a sincere "Welcome to our group!" I could also see their genuine kindness, I saw their caring nature, and I observed the compassion they had for one another and for me...but most of all, I could see clearly that they loved Jesus!

We introduced ourselves and I told them a little about me. They genuinely showed loving acceptance. I was amazed at their sincere efforts to make me feel at home. They accepted me and demonstrated an eagerness to do all they could to meet any need I had! They were and continue to be genuinely caring and actually practicing what the Bible says. During the months I attended, rarely missing any sessions, I never heard criticism of any other faith nor was there mention of any religious doctrine—they were so focused on learning the Word of God and to know Jesus in a deeper way. I felt right at home because that was also the desire of my heart.

During the times we spent studying the Word of God, I opened my heart to them, and they did the same thing. Consequently, we have become close friends. As a matter of fact, one of them came to me after a meeting once and said, "I want to take you home tonight. I just want to talk to you and spend some time with you. Everyone else wants to take you home and I want my turn!" This is an example of the loving nature of each of these ladies! We began to gather for social events as well as in each other's homes. They became my family.

19

Following God's Lead

"Attend church somewhere else? That would be a serious offense to the doctrine of my religion!" The old record played over and over in my mind.

During the two years I faithfully attended the weekly Bible study, I bonded with my new Christian friends so much that I considered all of them my family. From time to time they would invite me to the Sunday worship service, but I politely declined.

I feel that if I'm going to tell my story, I need to be completely honest with myself and with those who read it. My new life in Jesus, my convictions about what I believed, as well as my commitment to the Word of God, had come a long, long way. I consistently made every effort to make sure that my growth continued, and it most definitely did, mostly as a result of the encouragement I received from my new Christian friends.

For some reason...perhaps it was fear of changing something I had been doing all my life, I still continued to attend the same church on Sundays.

"Do I have to go?" asked our sons every Sunday. "I don't

get anything out of it!" they complained. I was hurt, disappointed, and at a loss of what to do. The worst part was that I, too, had come to a point where my Sunday attendance had become more of a ritual than the worship that touched my heart and drew me closer to Christ. I often found myself repeating the responses with my mouth, but my mind and heart were elsewhere. My attendance had become a comfortable habit rather than a challenge to live my life differently.

Making a change, however, would mean being the object of unfair judgment. There was a time when I did the very same thing—judged those who left "my faith" as if they had committed a serious offense. I wasn't then, but I am now very much aware of God's response to that type of judgment, "Hypocrite! First remove the plank from your own eye, and then you will see clearly to remove the speck out of your brother's eye" (Matthew 7:5 NKJV).

Once I was able to understand that God doesn't require me to belong to a religion in order to have a personal relationship with Him, I put everything into perspective. I realized that too much emphasis is put on names of denominations. I often question whether God judges me by what I'm called—Catholic, Baptist, Presbyterian, Methodist, etc.—or will He judge me by where my heart is and my level of commitment to the written Word of God, which is the only way I came to know Jesus, the *Living* Word of God.

I never reached a point in my walk with Jesus where I could say that I felt like I knew all there is to know, or I felt that God had done all He could in my life. Instead, I continued to seek a closer relationship with Him in every aspect. This included worshiping Him on a deeper and more meaningful level. I am certain that God read my heart because He honored this desire, "So I say to you, ask, and it will be given to you; seek, and you will find; knock, and it will be opened to you" (Luke 11:9 NKJV). God answered my prayer once again and opened the door to the church where

I could have the opportunity to worship as my heart longed for. I was again invited to the Sunday service. This time I accepted. I saw what I'd missed by not accepting this invitation long ago when they extended it to me the first time! I had missed opportunities to worship with a passion I had not known before. This kind of worship focused on the biblical principles by referring directly to what God's Word says. It put rituals aside and created a hunger and thirst for the knowledge of Jesus Christ.

When I initially mentioned to Gene that I wanted to attend this worship service, his response was "Sure." I wasn't certain what that meant. Did he mean "Sure, go right ahead," or "Sure, I can't understand it, but I support you," or "Sure, but just don't ask me to do that!" Whatever he meant, I know that I had his full support because, from the very beginning, he had so lovingly encouraged me in every step of my spiritual walk. I was certain that this was no exception, even though I wasn't about to imply that he follow my same path.

Sunday came, and he dropped me off at the new church and he went on to the one we had been attending. The next Sunday, we both attended the old church but afterwards he dropped me off to attend the other service. Each time I worshiped God on this deeper level, which was still very new to me, I would come home and share with Gene all I had learned, as well as tell him about the passion with which the congregation demonstrated their love for God!

I also told him that this worship was not just an emotional experience, a "good" feeling that came over me and then vanished after leaving the building. God had really touched my heart in a way that I knew without a doubt that His hand was in this. Because I knew God and my husband intimately, I knew better than to push, nag, coax, or insinuate to Gene that he should do anything. I let God work in his heart. I gently told him that if he ever wanted to join me I would be very happy. His answer was a polite "No, thanks."

That was perfectly fine with me because at least he didn't say, "I have my own faith." Even though I have, with an attitude similar to that of the Scribes, said that statement myself at one time or another. I have to admit that I wasn't sure what that phrase really meant.

After a while, Gene did accept the invitation to attend the service I valued so much. His reaction was very similar to mine. We both have commented and shared our amazement at God's provision in bringing us to this place of worship in a manner that feeds us spiritually. The worship through music in our new church often moves us to the point of bringing tears to our eyes as well as tears of joy.

Pastor John's sermons are full of insight, truths, and explanations of scripture, which are applicable to our lives. His style, sprinkled with humor and examples drawn from his own life, always point to the Word of God. Our hearts are touched because his passion for Jesus and compassion for others is contagious; so much so that Gene and I have a renewed desire to know the Lord by hearing His Word with more conviction than ever. I find that it is an absolute blessing for Gene and me to share the same hunger for Jesus and grow in our faith together!

Attendance in our new church has also made a difference for our sons. When our boys come to church to worship with us, they do so now with an open and positive attitude. They have shared with us that they now hear messages that make sense to them. We still receive communion together; the difference now is that they are getting to really know the Jesus they received on a personal level. Not only do they come on their own but they have also invited their girlfriends and other friends. I celebrate with joy in my heart knowing that my sons refer to the Bible on their own initiative.

Personal Message

"My hero!" is my loving and grateful response to Gene as he, for the umpteenth time has come to my rescue. He has in the almost thirty years of marriage found items which I dropped or simply couldn't find, guided me around potentially dangerous objects, shopped with me, run an endless number of errands for me - the list goes on and on. But what is most admirable about him is the creative ways he comes up with to make my life easier.

As a rule, I never take my white cane when we go out. It gets in the way and I find no need for it. Someone always accompanies me, and it's easier to rely on his or her assistance. Gene and I like to go out alone to a variety of places, such as restaurants, on a regular basis. Once in a while, I need to use the ladies room and, of course, Gene has to walk me to the door. He naturally has to stand right by the door so as to grab my hand when I come back out. No doubt that he is the object of strange looks by those ladies who don't know his real reason for standing and staring at the bathroom door. Knowing him, he probably just smiles shyly as he stands guard, waiting for his blind bride to come out.

But here is when he demonstrates not only his devotion, but his unique way to help me out. I mean really help me out. When he notices that I have taken longer than usual, he assumes (and he is always right) that I am having difficulty finding the door to exit. Often when there is no one inside the bathroom for me to ask for assistance, I need to resort to the only thing left to do—to literally "feel" my way out. Gene is very much aware of this, so in order to make this search easier for me, he taps on the door from the outside. While inside, I hear that tap. Aha! I now know which direction to take my steps. In a matter of moments, voila! I find the door...I open it confidently and reach out for the security of his strong and familiar hand.

147

When I hear that tap, it's a familiar sound and I know exactly what it means. It's familiar because it was meant only for me. Anyone else listening would dismiss the sound as unimportant.

So often, the Word of God has spoken to me with a similar, familiar tap on my heart, a calling that seems to be directed right to me. I know that I need to obey it and follow its direction. One of these "taps" of my heart was coming from the clear instructions given by Jesus. This was the call to be baptized. My initial reaction was to rely on the fact that I had obeyed this instruction by my baptism as a child. But the repentance that God's Word clearly instructs was not part of this commitment. "Then Peter said to them, Repent, and let everyone of you be baptized in the name of Jesus Christ for the remission of sins; and you shall receive the gift of the Holy Spirit" (Acts 2:38 NKJV).

I wondered, "Hmmm...what part of 'repent,' don't you understand?"

Baptism was not a suggestion or an option if I wanted to be truly committed to Him—a commitment not to a religion or denomination but to God. Gene's and my baptism at our new church was a physical representation of what God had done in our lives spiritually. Taking this step was important because we both wanted to comply with what Jesus so clearly indicated.

God knows all. He knew that our family needed to be spiritually prepared and equipped with the knowledge of His Word in order to face what was about to take place.

20

Unthinkable Tragedy

I would like to ask you to stop reading for a moment and pause for a few seconds. If you would close the book long enough to search your heart for any burden you carry...big or small. The reason this is necessary is because rather than just an observer, I would like you to accompany me down the path of restoration, one that I followed as it was led by Jesus taking me to complete victory.

I'm sure that you remember that my journey began with skepticism, doubt, and uncertainty. You saw the changes. It eventually turned to a deep conviction, coming from the depth of my soul. It affected me to such an extent that it drastically had to affect my relationship with Jesus as well as the relationship with others around me. It also drastically affected the stability of my emotions. My relationship with Him also completely changed the way in which I faced positive or extremely painful experiences in life.

The following episode is one that I hope will illustrate the sustaining power of God in the midst of inexpressible sorrow.

It was Sept. 7, 2002, at 2:30 in the morning, when the

phone rang. A few moments later our middle son Jeff abruptly entered our room to inform us that Joe was badly hurt. As Gene and I frantically rushed out the door, my heart and mind began to live the most grueling episode of my life. Jeff, Gene, and I drove to the hospital where Joe had been taken. The ambulance had already arrived, and they informed us that "They were working on him."

My desperation was overwhelming and impossible to describe. Once in the emergency room, we received the heart-wrenching news that Joe had not made it. There are no words in any language or dialect to express the ripping and crashing pain to a mother's heart as she hears the news that she has lost a child.

Our terrifying ordeal began. The detectives informed us that Joe was stabbed. He had been in a confrontation with a man at our local 7-11 convenience store. They were doing what they could to apprehend the other man. We were not concerned with any of those details because Gene and I were doing all we could to maintain our sanity. Although not audible, my heart held cries of horror, disbelief, and denial. These cries to God were really telling Him that I did not want this to happen. This was not fair! This pain was not deserved nor accepted by me. I was focusing on my own devastation, while disregarding God's power and faithfulness to me.

My human mind saw this as the worst violent storm that could ever be imagined. This storm was formed by winds of unbearable pain, caused by the rough waters of anguish, brutally tossed about by feelings of helplessness, as my heart was torn by the crashing violence of the waves of disbelief of what had happened to my child. I felt insignificant in the midst of the immense sea of agony bigger than anything I could handle.

Where was my strong faith and confidence in the midst of this terrifying storm? I found the answer by remembering His Word, which says, "...be still and know that I am God."

Once I realized that a living God, full of mercy and comfort, was in control, I could refocus on Him to soften the impact of such an event.

My heart was torn as if there was nothing left to hang on to, but my mind held his Word loud and clear: "My grace is sufficient" (2 Corinthians 12:9; see also Psalm 91:15).

God had sustained me through His Word before, and I could be sure that He would do the same at this moment of desperation.

The funeral arrangements and the burial were extremely painful. Gene and I, together with Jason and Jeff took the steps necessary to comply with the burial traditions dictated by this society. As the four of us—and the harsh reality was that now there were only four of us—walked to the car parked on the driveway, I listened to the birds singing. This was something I enjoyed and was always in tune to any time I stepped outside. But now, it was different. Everything was different. I suddenly disliked the sound. The birds' cheerful singing seemed so out of place, so did the warm sunshine. We got in the car; I could feel the heat from the sun radiating through the windows, quite a contrast to my heart and my world, which were dark, cold and gloomy without my youngest son. We rode silently to the funeral home to do something none of us would have ever dreamed we would be doing. All four of us were forced to take care of the most unpleasant, dreadful, and excruciating details of the funeral arrangements. This was so painfully opposite to what we were used to doing for Joe. It seemed as if events involving him had been a most pleasant and fun thing for us—going to watch his talents being displayed on the football and lacrosse fields. We would faithfully attend with anticipation to see him at his best. We also looked forward to hearing Joe's next witty and truly funny comment about anything especially when least expected.

We rode in silence. None of us knew exactly what was

going through each other's minds, or what degree of pain was destroying our hearts. Although inside we were sobbing, inside the car we just heard silence. At this point, I did something I had always done while riding in the car when our sons were small. While they were in the back seat, I would turn to them and give them some treat or toy to quiet them down. I guess that instinct was still in me at that time because I turned toward the back where Jason and Jeff sat, quietly torn apart by their pain. Although I knew this time that there was nothing, absolutely nothing, I could hand to them in order to make their anguish go away, but I still tried. I turned and said to them, "Know what I think? If Joe were here, he would be saying, 'Guys, let me put it to you this way, I'm in a great place! Remember how much I hated to get up early for work or school? Got good news for you. Up here… you never have to do that." I couldn't tell if they were smiling; they probably weren't. I wasn't Joe; I wasn't funny.

"How we could use Joe's wit and insightful comments right about now," I wished silently. He always had an unexpected remark to diffuse any amount of tension. When he was six years old, I had taken them to a shopping mall with a fountain in the middle. As they saw others do, Joe and his brothers wanted to throw coins in it. As I approached the edge to hand them the coins, I got a little too close and fell right in. It wasn't deep, so I quickly stepped out, hoping no one noticed me. I was soaked, and with the shock, I had neglected to notice that my sunglasses, which I had placed on the top of my head, had flown off. Joe proceeded to jump in, retrieve them, run over to me and, with a tone of authority mixed with a certain amount of scolding, said to me, "Mom, next time you want to go swimming, please let me know first!"

Joe grew up and so did his unique sense of humor to make anyone laugh with incomparable insight. He seemed to know what one needed at any given moment. But now we were headed to take the steps that would be the tangible but cruel reminder that Joe was not with us anymore. We had to reluctantly move on. Once in the funeral home, the director said to Gene with cordiality and respect, "Here is the price range for the coffins. Please look it over and let me know." He paused and added, "If you like, you can step in that room and choose the one you like best."

How can you "like" the coffin your child would be buried in? What criteria do you use in order to choose such a thing? With each piece of information and question that needed to be answered, it was as if he were hurling a bucket of ice water on my face. Before I could catch my breath, he was throwing another one at me with a cruelty unknown to him.

As difficult as this process was, I maintained my serenity and peace. I no longer had Joe and his ability to make me laugh. But I still had Jesus. He would be the only one who could bring back the joy and the laughter. That, I was absolutely certain of. It would take time, perhaps a long, long time! For the moment, all I could do was to lean on Jesus. Consequently, the outward composure and strength I displayed was the reflection of the peace I held in the depth of my heart; one which I obtained directly from Him. This was His promise to me, "The LORD is my rock and my fortress and my deliverer; My God, my strength, in whom I will trust" (Psalm 18:2).

21

My Own Time Line

The anguish that took my breath away became unbearable when I focused solely on my human view of all of this. I was in shock as I realized how Joe's death had destroyed my time line, the one that I had carefully but almost subconsciously set for my life. I wanted my children to attend my burial; I did not want to bury my youngest son—or any of my children! I wanted to read in the newspaper about Joe's sports achievements, not the details of that violent act. I had planned to some day help pick out the tuxedo for his wedding, not the clothes he would be buried in. I wanted to choose the wording for his college graduation announcement, not the obituary text. I wanted to help pick out his first house, not his burial site. I still wanted to continue to hear Gene read to me passages from the Bible and devotionals for Christian married couples, not books for grieving parents.

These thoughts tormented me, and I felt alone and abandoned. It was only when my focus changed to God that peace filled my heart. I could see clearly that Jesus also did not want to do a lot of the things He faced. This is more evident to me when I put aside my own self-desires or wants for the way life should be. I can then focus on and learn from Jesus' submission to suffering.

Jesus did not want to suffer, or to be tortured and ridiculed as He was. Nor did He want to wear the crown of thorns piercing His head. He did not want to be nailed onto a wooden cross. He did not choose to be tortured every step leading up to His death.

The only reason why He endured this pain was to pay for our sins and, in so doing, accept God's will. When He did, He knew the glory that awaited Him. For me, to accept what happened to Joe would also mean that I am willing to accept God's will. With my acceptance of pain, I'm also accepting God's compassion, His comfort, His sustaining power, and His faithful love that brings new hope even in the midst of desperation and sorrow. God did not cause this violent act. It was the evil in this world that brought it about, but I'm also willing to accept the promises that God will turn to good whatever Satan meant for evil.

What If

The unavoidable questions are ever present in the midst of tragedies. In our situation, the "what if" questions surfaced as a result of us believing for a moment that we or Joe could have done something...*anything*...different to avoid him going home when he did. In thinking this way, what we are really implying is that in some way we could have been in control rather than God. But in the back of our minds, the questions persist: What if Joe had not been out that night? What if we hadn't moved to Florida? What if Joe had gone away to college? What if he had not pulled into that 7-11? What if?

I will try to answer these with yet other questions, but ones that have a clear answer in scripture.

What if the living God had not shown His mercy but instead chose to allow physical death, including Joe's, to be the end? What if God had not sent His only son Jesus to die for us and thus give us eternal life? What if we had to be "good" in order to enter heaven...I would be forever asking if Joe was "good" enough. What if Joe had not made the commitment to Christ and accepted Him as his Savior at a young age?

Another question is ever present in the mind of those who suffer this pain with us. Why did God take Joe at such a young age? I would never attempt to understand God's ways. If I understand life as a Christian at all, the fact is everyone, without exception, will face physical death in God's perfect timing. The only difference is that for those who know Jesus Christ as their Savior, physical death is most definitely *not* the end! Rather, each day on this earth leads not to death but to eternal life. At times, the Bible calls us by a very fitting name "sheep." I guess it's because sheep are not the most intelligent animals...and some of us aren't either. Jesus refers to himself as "our Shepherd." As our shepherd he assures us:

"My sheep hear my voice, and I know them, and they follow me. And I give them eternal life, and they shall never perish; neither shall anyone snatch them out of My hand." (John 10:27-28 NKJV)

Joe knew Jesus' voice and chose to follow Him. He was by no means perfect. He had many faults, but no matter what he went through, Joe could not be "plucked out" of His loving hand. For this reason Joe, as well as all of those who follow the call from our protective shepherd, have the guarantee of eternal life. Consequently, just as Joe, those of us who follow Jesus don't live to die, but die each day, looking forward to eternal life. The last word for a Christian is not death, but life...eternal life!

Although we desired to have Joe outlive us, God called

him according to His divine timing and not ours. For this reason, Joe's funeral service was one of celebration, the rejoicing of his entrance to the glory of heaven. Those of us left here on earth are the ones who need to face the ups and downs of emotions, including our natural grief over someone who has left us. But with the Lord, these emotions can be put into perspective. The moments that might cause us to shed tears are ones that are necessary to heal and are ones that express how much I miss Joe. God is aware of all. He said that we are blessed because we mourn ...why would He say that we are blessed? Listen to what follows as His promise: "Blessed are those who mourn, for they shall be comforted" (Matthew 5:4 NKJV).

Yes, He promised comfort. And the comfort given by Jesus, the Lord of all, can be one that sustains one through any unthinkable tragedy. It was this comfort, provided by a loving God, which enabled me to move forward with confidence.

Some might be asking: How can this woman find good things to talk about? How can she still have joy and be able to laugh? How can she possibly go through life with enjoyment and without debilitating sorrow? The answer is given to me and to you in this verse: "I can do all things through Christ who strengthens me" (Philippians 4:13 NKJV).

There are three key words in this particular verse. They are, "Christ," "all," and "strength." If "Christ" were not there, then, it would mean that I would be alone, able to do nothing. If the word "all" weren't there, it would mean that Christ would only be able to strengthen me in some areas and not in others. And finally, if the word "strength" were to be removed, it would mean that I would be left at the mercy of my human weakness—left helpless and hopeless.

My heart echoes with conviction over and over again, "I can do all things through Christ who strengthens me." This is not just a religious phrase suited for repetition. It is most definitely the powerful promise of God, a promise that is not only reassuring but also, relevant and real.

As I've explained, it was God who made it possible for me to survive this episode. It's more important, however, to show you also what lies on the other side of a tragedy. Among the reflections in Part II, I'll explain how Jesus turned this episode around, how He turned the darkness brought on by sorrow to the light brought on by His love.

My Mom, Dad, Ed & I in 1964

My Mom, Dad, Ed and I in 2004

My Family, Joe, Gene, Myself, Jason & Jeff

My three J's – Jason, Joe & Jeff

Joe's High School Graduation 2001

Joe Eckles
(October 19, 1982 – September 7, 2002)

PART II

MY REFLECTIONS

Introduction

You've read the first half of my story. The better part is yet to come. It will be presented to you in a slightly different format, in order to bring to light the reasons for each event in my journey. In Part I, you and I have walked through the steps that took me around corners, finding joyful as well as painful detours. The unavoidable happened—great gains and horrid losses—with each step of my journey forcing me to see life differently. As a result, I filled the "see" drive of my heart with large files of lessons learned, insights gained, priorities re-arranged; but more importantly—irrefutable truths were drawn from the Word of God.

What purpose does all this stored information serve? The only one who could give the answer to that is you. It will depend on what you decide to do as you scroll down each file, whether you choose to delete them from your memory or save them in the files of your heart. Even if you decide to save some of them in your temporary file for future reference, the purpose of sharing my story with you was well served!

Now that you have a hint of what the next pages contain, allow me to take a few steps ahead of you. I will take the handle of the door, open it gently, and invite you to come in. Come in to the den of my heart where the intimate files are stored. I reserved a place just for you. Make yourself comfortable on the seat next to me. I will hand you a cup of insights, sweetened with anecdotes, with a touch of humor for flavor. I'll put before you a platter of warm reflections prepared by God in the oven of my heart. They will be garnished with sincerity, candor and truth. No need to worry about calories—it's nutritious food to strengthen your soul!

22

Answers

Did you notice the surge of books that include the words, "...for Dummies?" How about this title? *The Manual for Overcoming Adversity for Dummies*. I guess that would have been an option for a title for my book. But how could I write a book for "dummies" if I was a dummy myself! A dummy because there was a time when I thought I knew all the answers...actually I did know life's important answers — the only problem was that they were all the wrong ones.

The painful events in my life became the rigorous true or false test I was forced to take. I had to learn what was true and what was false. This time, however, I got 100 percent correct...an "A!" All right...I cheated, I peeked at the textbook (the Bible). There I found each of the answers spelled out for me.

I think that it would be fair to divide most people into two categories: Those who have only questions about life, and those who seem to have all the answers (I'll add a third one – those who don't care.)

"Finding yourself" is the popular theme of self- books. "Please yourself first" rings out as the tempting invitation to reach complete satisfaction. "Be a good person" seems to be the ultimate goal of many.

Have you embraced any of these popular philosophies? Did you find the answers you were looking for? Perhaps you never took the time to even think about it at all. Well...I have! Not only have I thought about the entire list above, but, as I've said, I tried, at one time or another, to live up to them all.

Here is how I learned the correct answers; somehow, they blatantly contradict the ones I had known!

"I'd hate to have a house built!" announced my friend when I told her that Gene and I were thinking about building one.

"It's so hard to make up your mind about colors, layout of the house, design, and dealing with builders...it's a pain!" she added with annoyance in her voice.

I found that building a house is one of those experiences that you either love or hate. Gene and I happen to love each stage of this process. I was still sighted at the time we built our first home. We were thrilled to pick out all brand new items, from the bathroom fixtures to the outside lights. Therefore, when the decision to build our next home was made, I was excited and looked forward to the same experience! Oops! There was one slight difference, however, I was now without sight!

As one of the first steps in building the new house, Gene and I decided to have it custom designed to our specifications. We chose a particular builder because they offered, as part of their incentive, a decorator who would work with us. The decorator helped coordinate the colors, fixtures, and general theme of the home.

"Let's see, Jan, which shade of green do you think would be best for the window shutters?" Would that be a question I could answer? Would I end up being frustrated at my inability to make decisions that were at one time enjoyable for me? Would I just be setting myself up for a disappointment...should I look to other more reasonable options?

My decision was made. Go forward with this project. Why? Because I was now guided by a new set of values. I was determined to accomplish whatever I chose to do, sighted or not. My heart now held this confidence because I was trusting in God's guidance in small and big things. They ranged from picking out colors for our new home to choosing whether to feel self-pity or feel incredibly blessed to have God in my life.

As the construction began, Gene and I would visit the site as often as we could. We looked forward with anticipation to seeing the progress. We made sure to take periodic trips to check the construction. Initially there was not much there but some uneven ground with dirt and rocks. There were partial pieces of wood and construction material left everywhere. This was understandable because the builders were still in the process of doing their work. Cleaning up was the last step that came after the completion. But it also meant that Gene had to carefully lead me through the debris.

Through the years, Gene has shown his patience in so many ways. He displayed this quality once again. He would repeatedly explain to me the layout of the house: the location of the rooms, their size, the arrangement of the appliances in the kitchen, etc. He wanted me to have a picture of what the whole thing would look like. This was important because I wanted to know just how the furniture would fit. As he held my hand on the table, he would use my fingers to trace an imaginary map of the interior. His explanations would begin with, "Pretend that this is where the kitchen is, and pretend this is the..." This allowed me to visualize the house well enough to determine where the electric outlets should be placed. I could do this because in my mind, I already had an idea of the arrangement of the furniture.

The fun part for me was getting closer. Working with the

decorator to pick out colors, patterns, and designs was a great thrill for me. She gave me choices and options that I would either approve or reject. She was patient with me as I asked her to describe details that I'm sure she never had to do with any other client she had. At one point, she suggested one of the greatest features I thought had been invented. She told me about a style of windows that contained the blinds inside the windowpanes. This would eliminate the cleaning because they were protected from dirt and would be opened and closed using a small knob on the outside. I liked blinds because I could control the amount of light coming in—the more light the better. For most, a window is simply a part of a house, but for me it is the only guide I have. The light coming from a window gives me the point of reference necessary to walk confidently throughout the house.

Finally, it was ours. "Sign here," said Gene, guiding the pen above the paper toward the direction I needed to put my signature. As I scribbled my name on numerous papers along with Gene's, the home was ours!! Was it really? Or was it the banks? Simply because we held keys and had access to it didn't make us the true owners. It most definitely belonged to the financial institution.

As we began to enjoy our brand new home, the bank also enjoyed receiving our sizable mortgage payment checks. Of course, initially our payments were used mostly to cover the loan's interest. We joined the rest of Americans who fall into the slavery to a master called mortgage. Gene and I were committed to work hard in order to make the payments on time. The bank had the power because failure to comply with this commitment on our part would result in foreclosure.

By now you know me well enough to predict what I am about to do, right? Anything, which seems mundane such as building a house, holds for me some deep meaning. This is no exception. The stages of this process brought to light answers to some questions I had before I began my walk with Jesus.

The Bible calls the debris of the heart "sin." The cleaning up is a needed process, but, unlike with our house, it's not the last step; it's the first. The cleanser used is the blood that Jesus shed at the cross. All that is needed is to genuinely repent, receive Him, and be forgiven.

A house without windows to allow the sunlight to come in would be a dark gloomy place, much like a prison. Similarly, a life without the light of the Word of God to provide the brightness of His love can be a spiritually cold and dark cell. Its darkness makes it impossible to "find yourself."

This is another answer I found. Gene would have me pretend to know the location of the various rooms in our partially built home in order for me to have an idea of its layout. Likewise, there was a time when I was in the "pretend" stage of my life as well. I was eager to please everyone around me, first my parents, then my teachers, then my friends, my husband, and even my children. I guess in the end I didn't really know whom to please; even worse I thought that I was pleasing myself by pleasing them! So I pretended that I was making them all happy at one time or another.

But the only problem was that as I strived to please them, I wasn't being rewarded in proportion to my giving. So I *pretended* to be satisfied, to be "complete." But I really wasn't. So what was the problem...isn't that the job of a wife and mother to make the family the first priority? Here was my answer: "Master, which is the great commandment in the law? Jesus said unto him, Thou shalt love the Lord thy God with all thy heart, and with all thy soul, and with all thy mind" (Matthew 22:36-37).

The missing piece of the puzzle was put in place. Then the priorities were finally in line correctly, making the first one very clear. I made Jesus the first focus of my energy, my efforts, my work, and my service. Pleasing Him gave me the freedom to stop pretending to have what I really didn't and to turn to Him for answers. When I was drained, He strengthened me. When I was lost, He gave me clear direction. When I was confused, He provided clear direction. When I was taken for granted, He let me know that I was special and loved. When I wanted to fit in, He gave me reassurance that He accepted me no matter what. The wisdom He gave me allowed me to put the right priorities in line, to give unselfishly, and to be refueled by His love. Drawing from this endless resource gave me all I needed to become the best wife, mother, friend, Sunday school teacher, employee, etc. The gauge I use to determine what "best" really is did not come from the world's standards. It came from God…making Him first can only bring the best results.

Consequently, there is no need to pretend to have, to be, or to feel anything. It's sufficient to have a genuine desire to please God and Him alone. When I did, I gained the freedom to be just who I was—His child totally dependent on Him!

Although we held the keys to our house, we really weren't the true owners—it was the bank that owned and had control of it. Although we hold the free will to make our own decisions, God is ultimately in control. Initially I had gone on my own. When faced with a crisis, I was headed for despair. Looking to Jesus allowing Him to take control, He redirected my steps toward something good.

It was obviously necessary for us to take care of our house. We had the responsibility to clean it and repair it when needed. However, doing this would not keep it from foreclosure. Similarly, all the good deeds we might do as a "good person" will not keep us from eternal death.

Many years of following the scheduled payments for the mortgage resulted in the house finally becoming "ours." God offers all of us a mansion in Heaven. What is the payment schedule for this residence? There is none…it's a gift! The reason it's a gift is because God offers it. He is not selling it. The only string attached is the one connecting your heart with His!

23

The Other Side

"I'd like to ask you one more thing." This request became part of any flight reservation I made. "I'm blind and will need assistance to make my connection." The reservations clerks are all very accommodating and courteous whenever I make this request. My blindness could have been a reason to let my limitations hold me prisoner. But when I began walking with Jesus, I discovered that the contrary was true. I found more courage and confidence to undertake ventures, ones that I might not have even thought of while sighted.

Traveling is one of those activities I enjoy very much. I have gone to South America and back and from Florida to California by myself. These trips were not only enjoyable but also quite rewarding for me. In order to navigate through a crowded airport, I rely on the assistance of airport or airline personnel. This gives me the opportunity to meet and get to know interesting people. Even when I sit next to someone, he or she is not a stranger for very long. I take advantage of any opportunity to strike a conversation and share stories. Often the door opens for me to go into some detail about my blindness and what God has done in my life. This seems to come about naturally because people are often curious. Eventually they want to know more about me. After some small talk, they hesitantly ask,

"Were you born blind?" or "Are you completely blind?"

The reason they ask this is because, as people have commented before, I don't "look" blind. Since I was sighted a good part of my life, I naturally turn my head toward the person speaking. As I follow the person's voice, I focus my eyes on them even when I can't really see any image. Consequently, often it's difficult for those who don't know me to determine whether I have some sight or not. I guess it's because I always try to wear make-up, including some carefully placed eyeliner. This adds to their puzzling thoughts as they wonder if I'm really blind.

Here's a side note just for ladies. If someone were to ask me what is the question that I am asked most often, I'd have to answer that it would be the one about my make-up—they all want to know just how does a blind person put on her make-up? It's simple. After all, what is the motivator? Vanity! That is the honest answer! So, since I have the necessary motivator, I go to work. Also, since I don't need a light or mirror, I can put it on anywhere, anytime. I have all my eye shadows placed inside specific places in my compact. I know the exact number of strokes of each shade—one that goes on the crease of the eyelid and the other is for highlighting. The lips and blush? Same thing, I make sure that only the correct amount of strokes go on the brush, feel the cheekbones and the lips.

The eyeliner? I can feel my eyelashes and that is my guide, one smooth stroke and voila! The mascara? Well, it's difficult to miss my eyelashes. Finally, I make sure that I dab a little eye moisturizer around the eye, because this does two things; it wipes any smear around the eye and keeps that area moisturized. There! Finished product! Gene always gives me his final approval as well. There have been times when I went a little too heavy and my sweet husband informed me of that fact in a tactful and loving way! Now, back to my traveling experiences

Although most of my traveling experiences are rewarding, I have had some embarrassing moments. On one of those trips, I was coming back from San Diego. This time, Gene was with me. As we waited for the airplane to take off, I was settled in the middle seat. Gene was to my left in the aisle seat. After a few moments, a dear lady made her way through the tight space in front of me and sat to my right next to the window. Once she settled down, I began my usual way of starting a conversation. I began to ask simple questions about her travels. She responded by relating a lengthy and detailed story about a convention, which she had just attended. She didn't give me the opportunity to share anything about myself, which was fine with me. I was fascinated by what she was telling me. I was listening attentively as she went on and on about the details of her adventure. I was intrigued with her passion and hobby of collecting these unique items. Without taking a break in her story, she proceeded to root through her bag. With an enthusiastic tone, she said to me, "Here is a picture of my grandbaby with one of my collectibles."

I paused, realizing that I had to quickly make a choice. One would be to tell this nice lady that I was blind. If I had done so, she would have undoubtedly been embarrassed as she learned that she was showing a picture to a blind person. In an effort to avoid any awkward explanations, I chose to hold out my hand. Looking down at the picture, I proceeded to make the usual polite remarks, "Awe...that is so cute, its adora..." Before I could finish the sentence, Gene quickly took my hand and adjusted the picture. His swift move was to remedy the situation—I had been looking at the back of the picture!

As trivial as this incident may seem, it held a deeper meaning regarding the transformation of my life. Similar to the back of that picture, my life, without Jesus, was empty. Although it was full of activities, it was incomplete and insipid. In my effort to conform or fit into the world's mold, I was looking for fulfillment in what it had to offer or in what I could do for myself. But rather than a soul-deep fulfillment, I found short-lived satisfaction, which only created a new desire to go after the next elusive goal. This endless cycle was a result of my inability to see beyond what Jesus had in store for me. Just as Gene turned the picture around, Jesus turned my life around. It now reflected color, richness, dimension, and lasting joy. There was no need to look for fulfillment. His abundance is more than enough to meet every need and desire. What is the key? The answer is simple, the Word of God says that to "turn around" or be transformed. "And do not be conformed to this world, but be transformed by the renewing of your mind, that you may prove what is that good and acceptable and perfect will of God" (Romans 12:2 NKJV).

Out with the Old, In with the New

"Can I ask you a favor?" whispered Mario as he gave me a great big hug wishing me a Happy New Year.

Mario had been a close friend of ours and sometimes he had goofy ideas. I wondered what that favor could be.

"Sure." I answered.

"Do you have a bucket?" he asked with a serious tone in his voice.

It was just a few moments after midnight and he was about to follow a tradition, dating back from years ago in his country.

"What do you need a bucket for?" I asked with curiosity as I handed him an old one I had found in the garage.

"You'll see," he replied as he held the bucket under the kitchen faucet. He filled it up with water. "It's a tradition;" he explained as I followed him through the front door. He got to the grass area, held the bucket with both hands and hurled it forward empting the bucket. The water made one big and loud splash all over the grass. "There!" he exclaimed with satisfaction, as if he had fulfilled a very important duty. "We throw the water out and with it, all the bad stuff from the previous year," he explained. "Now we're ready for all the good stuff to come in the New Year!"

Little did he know that the Bible has a similar concept— out with the old stuff and in with the new stuff. It's referred in the above verse as "transformation." The instruction is not to conform to this world but to be transformed by renewing your mind. This "renewal" implies that something has to go in order to have something else come in. In my walk with Christ, the same had to occur. I needed to let go and throw out the "old" way of thinking. It was time to throw out the limited amount of wisdom drawn from everywhere else but the Bible. For example, I used to think that by being a "good" person, I was certainly fulfilling the requirements to enter into heaven. But here is the problem, how good is "good?" I wasn't Mother Teresa, but I wasn't Hitler either, so what level of "good" was I? The reason that this question is so difficult to answer is because I had no way to measure the level of good or bad. I had no concrete point of reference, no solid and objective guideline. What made it even more complex is that we live in a culture dictated by the "it's all relative" mentality. Therefore, if I had a couple of abortions, but volunteered for the homeless, caused no harm to anyone, and was limited to one traffic violation every five years…would that mean I was a good person? This subjective way of thinking had to go out, leaving room for something new and better. I now held something, which replaced it. A new set of rules, new guidelines, new reliable points of reference.

When Jesus enters a heart like He did mine, a wonderful process begins. A hunger and thirst to know Him through His Word becomes the motivation and driving force to seek Him. This diligence to do that is rewarded by obtaining God's wisdom. This wisdom becomes essential in order to recognize the old and inaccurate values. They need to be thrown out just like Mario threw out the bucket of water on that New Year's Eve. "Therefore if any man be in Christ, he is a new creature: old things are passed away; behold, all things are become new" (2 Corinthians 5:17).

Learning with Your Heart

Did anyone ever ask you if you know your social security number by heart? To know something by heart means that you took time to memorize it. It's not just any bit of information that came and went from your mind. It's something that went to the next level—your heart. When a transformed mind and heart is filled with God's truth, unlike any piece of trivial information, His word becomes part of you—like your name, your birth date, etc., so much so that in any given moment, no matter what the circumstance, it naturally resounds loudly drowning any other piece of inaccurate information. A transformed believer holds God's truth not just in the mind but in the heart.

But what does that 'transformation' really mean as it relates to my life as a blind person? What it means is that in order for me to move forward according to God's perfect will, my mind needed to be renewed. It needed to change, so much so that I could leave behind this hang up of my physical blindness. It means that I no longer need to see it as a challenge, an impairment, or a handicap. It is not a challenge but a channel through which God's light shines through, allowing me to see my world with new eyes. It is most definitely not an impairment, but an improvement in my attitude, turning it into a positive one so that I can see beyond my physical limitations and focus on God's limitless abundance. It is certainly not a handicap but a handy tool held in Christ's hand to carve away and discard self-pity, anger, or bitterness, bringing forth the contour of a soul shaped with peace.

24

No More Chasing!

"I'm sorry, honey." That was probably the hardest thing for me to say to Gene. Saying it meant I was wrong and he was right – tough thing for my pride to swallow. But as hard as that was, it was part of my homework – work hard at applying God's Word into my home life.

I became a diligent student of the Word of God; consequently, the Bible became my textbook of life. It was the only one required as I enrolled in the university of spiritual growth. The only difference is that there is no graduation date...the learning never ends and the lessons are ongoing.

Speaking of learning, they say that hindsight is 20/20. I'll be the first one to agree with that! But now I know the reason why. Let me share with you the philosophy according to Jan. The reason that things seem clearer when we look back is because we can see what mistakes we made. Logically, by looking back, we can see what we could have done differently. Or we *should* be able to, if we've learned anything!

I believe the process of making decisions is divided into two categories. Which category would you fit into? In the first category are the decisions, big or small, which include

God's input. These decisions include the insight drawn from the Word of God. The second category contains decisions made excluding God's input. Each category has its own consequences. The ones made by following God's guidance have awesome results because they are so incredibly better than expected. The decisions made without God will result in disappointment and hardship. I know this because I've learned it first hand. I've shared with you just about everything about me, no reason to stop now; so here it goes.

You see, along with my attempts to improve my own life, I did my best to change others around me as well. Who was my first target? You guessed it—Gene. I was emphatically outspoken about his way of disciplining our sons. I saw deficiencies in his methods because they were so different from what I knew. I was brought up in a very strict and structured home. My style of raising our sons reflected these tendencies as well. I felt that our sons should have the same restrictions and limitations in their behavior, habits, and general demeanor. I tried and tried to make Gene see the light. I definitely wanted him to recognize his shortcomings so that we could be a team working together as we raised our sons. (Notice how the focus was on "me" and how "I" was seeing things?)

What were the results? Gene's style was different, he believed in giving the boys more freedom and somewhat less structure. The opposing views on these child-raising theories certainly caused painful divisions between us, more so than any other area in our relationship. On many occasions we each stood our ground so much that it resulted in hurtful feelings and alienation. My relentless insistence in getting my way certainly blocked me from being open to any other options to resolve this conflict.

This part is for the ladies. If any gentleman is reading this, you can go ahead and tune out the next couple of paragraphs. Since I'm being really, really honest with you, let me go on. Not only did I believe that Gene's childrearing ways were not up to my standards, but I also thought he lacked the spiritual convictions, the same ones that I had developed. So, what did I do? Possibly the same thing some of you have done—I tried and tried again and again to talk to him about what I knew and what he should do. Not that he was a heretic. On the contrary, he was a godly man already...but not godly enough for me. Some of you have been there? If so, here is my advice: First I would run to you quick as lightning, blow my whistle loudly, hold out my hand and shout, "Stop!" Trust me, I speak from experience. It will be for you just like it was for me.

It was like chasing a plastic cup...yes, you read it right, a plastic cup. It didn't take long before I realized that common sense had to be applied to many things I tried to do around the house. It ranged from small, insignificant things to bigger and more important ones. One of the more trivial instances was, for example, when I dropped something. It was evident that when I was alone and needed to pick up any item that fell on the floor, I had to come up with ways to find it on my own. So the first thing to do is to listen as the item falls and follow the sound. Doing this allows me to go to that general direction and begin to feel with my hands and find it. One day while in the kitchen, I dropped a plastic cup. I followed the correct steps: I listened, followed the sound, and attempted to retrieve it. But this time, it wasn't as easy. At the very moment that I would get close to it, my foot would kick it, sending it off bouncing across the floor.

The same method was taken by following the sound, and I would come close to it, but as soon as I began to bend over to get it, my foot would kick it again. I must have chased that cup for who knows how long. I was determined that the cup would not win—by then I was convinced that it had come to life and was making fun of me. Soon after, my sweet mom came into the kitchen to save the day. She proceeded to take a quick glance, spotted the cup under the table, picked it up and swiftly put it in its place. Logical scenario, don't you think? She could see it and I couldn't.

The same scenario, however, applied to Gene's heart. I, who couldn't see it, was chasing it, attempting to place it where I thought it needed to be, when in reality, God, who sees all, including Gene's heart, should be the one who needed to take over. Along with other areas of my spiritual development, I obtained wisdom, the gift of wisdom, which comes from God's Word. Putting this new gift into practice, I decided to let go and let God take over. So I began to love Gene just where he was and pray for him...pray so that he would be where I thought he should be? Not at all. My new wise way of thinking led me to pray for him so that his heart would be right where God wanted it to be!

God wasn't done yet. As I mentioned, when He is in the picture, the results are better than expected. Not only did our confrontations regarding our views of childrearing diminish, but also God put in our path ways to improve our relationship. These included weekend events such as marriage conferences sponsored by Family Life Ministries. Each time one is held in Orlando, we sign up. Why would we do it over and over again? I guess it's for the same reason that you change the oil in your car. As we apply the insights shared in these events, we lubricate the mechanism of our relationship.

With God in the center, we know whom to turn to for answers. We receive the fuel for our marriage while we're on our knees together in prayer.

Dancing

Some time ago, Gene and I had the opportunity to sign up for ballroom dance lessons. When it comes to dancing, Gene could take it or leave it. For me, on the other hand, dancing is something I have always enjoyed. In the past I have danced everything from Flamenco to disco to swing. So you know which one of us *really* wanted to sign up for these lessons, right? Our dance teacher, Cindy, was very good as she patiently demonstrated what we needed to do. She lined the men on one side and gave them specific instructions regarding the dance steps they need to take. Then she turned to the line of women and did the same thing. The partners were now ready to try to put this into practice following the rhythm of the music.

This was a lot of fun, especially as we learned quite a few dance moves. We also learned quickly that when we fail to take the steps specifically designed for each one of us...ouch! One foot, his or mine, would suffer the painful consequence!

Similarly, God in his Word has designed specific steps for each one of us to follow as it relates to our roles in our marriage. These instructions are crystal clear: "Wives, submit to your own husbands, as is fitting in the Lord" (Colossians 3:18 NKJV). The companion verse is just as clear: "Husbands love your wives, just as Christ also loved the church and gave Himself for her" (Ephesians 5:25 NKJV).

Did you notice each one, husband and wife, has very specific responsibilities and parts to play? It's much like dancing together. If one doesn't do what he or she is supposed to do, then they will be out of step and the consequences are definitely painful!

25

Forgiveness

"**D**ad, are you crazy?" asked Jeff with disbelief. I think you might agree with Jeff's reaction when you read this unfortunate scenario.

So often setbacks in life, although painful, can be used to build character. The only question is whether this character will ultimately be pleasing to God or one that will please the world.

By 1999, Gene had been working for his employer in Orlando for more than three years, and he felt that the time was right for him to leave and pursue a business venture. He started a small retail company, and by the year 2000, he had been running it for about fifteen months. At that time, his company had expanded and was operating several retail stores in central Florida. Through all the stages of the business development, we both learned a great deal about people as they affected the daily operations. Our three sons and Gene's parents, as well as my own parents, pitched in to help in various aspects of the operation.

"You're not going to believe what happened today!" Gene chuckled, but I could sense a hint of frustration in his voice. I knew to expect just about anything when it came to the daily operations of this business.

"What happened now?" I asked, bracing myself, not knowing what this could possibly be.

"Remember the compressor we chained to the tree for security?" he began explaining.

"Yes, you did that to keep it from being stolen as before," I answered quickly.

"Well...they took it anyway, sawed the tree down and took the compressor!"

Starting a business can be a difficult task full of challenges and struggles, big and small. Some which are more serious can negatively affect family relationships. The ups and downs of the financial aspect of the business caused a painful strain in our marriage. Since we both had our own ideas on how to proceed in the business, the stress and tension became at times, overwhelming. We found it difficult to play the role God intended for each of us. Nevertheless, we persevered and made the commitment to let Jesus be our guide. As a result, we saw how constant prayer, forgiveness, and love for God and for one another turned an extremely difficult episode into a stronger marriage relationship. For us, this was another fulfillment of God's promise, "And we know that all things work together for good to those who love God" (Romans 8:28).

The company was growing and although the majority of the employees were dedicated and hard-working individuals, there were a few who weren't reliable and who caused some problems and challenges for Gene. The worst situation was when he suspected that two of them had taken funds and merchandise from the stores. Gene took the steps to make sure that this was the case. He managed to identify which ones were to blame. After the official surveillance by detectives, they were caught red-handed. Once arrested, the signed confession revealed that they had taken $40,000. This was a significant financial setback for a young company.

I admire many qualities about Gene, but his obedience to God and his forgiving nature would be at the top. As would be expected, Gene did not react with vengeance, anger, or self-pity. He based his reaction and course of action on wisdom and common sense. He had to make a choice. He could pursue litigation against individuals who had no funds to pay back and get involved in endless court proceedings that might have led to dead ends. Or he could forgive them.

He chose to forgive, just as he had been forgiven of some debts that were incurred unexpectedly. The Bible says that we should be "bearing with one another, and forgiving one another, if anyone has a complaint against another; even as Christ forgave you, so you also must do" (Colossians 3:13 NKJV).

In a conversation with our son Jeff, Gene explained his reason for handling the situation the way he did. But Jeff's reaction was one that most people would have had. He believed that Gene should seek restitution by pressing charges. It was only right that he follow through until everything was paid back with interest. It seemed logical because what those employees had done was wrong and deserved to be punished. But the world's view and God's often don't coincide. This kind of forgiveness, or lack of it, is illustrated in Matthew 18:22-35, which relates the forgiveness granted to a man who rather than be grateful, in turn, sought immediate and full payment of a debt owed to him.

Gene felt that the people who took from him should know the principles he followed, which had, in turn, dictated his actions. Since they were from a foreign country and practiced a different religion, perhaps they wouldn't have understood why a person would not seek vengeance. Gene explained that we were Christians and proceeded to make a request from them. They readily complied. He first settled on an amount of money to be repaid, which would cause them to stretch but be affordable for them to pay. Although this amount was significantly less than the debt owed, it was important for them to understand that although forgiven, there is a consequence for sinful actions. He then asked them to obtain a Christian Bible and meet with him to review specific Scriptures. He worked with them to understand the error (sin) of what they had done, but, more importantly, to share with them that the God we serve is a forgiving God.

The recovery of the funds, however, did not compare to the valuable lesson Gene gave to our sons regarding forgiveness.

26

Lessons for My Sons

ᨦ

"I don't know how you do it, Jan!" commented a dear friend. "I get so down even with little things and you seem to have a positive attitude all the time. How do you do it?" she asked with sincerity in her voice.

"Practice." I answered without hesitation. I practice focusing on God's words of encouragement and hope.

They say that children learn some lessons that are taught and some that are "caught." I believe that our sons learned through both ways: Some lessons that we purposely taught them and others by our example, such as the one on overcoming negative situations. I had not let my blindness overcome my life or have a negative effect on what I attempted to accomplish. On the contrary, by putting Christ at the center of everything, I held on to a positive and optimistic outlook. This might have been the best example I could give my sons.

"I disagree with you," I said with cautious boldness to my friend. "I don't think that a good education is the most important goal for our children," I began my explanation.

"They could have a doctorate degree in the most sought-after field, but if they lack a solid spiritual foundation, their lives will crumble when faced with a crisis."

I felt that it was important for my sons to see that optimism and a positive outlook of life is drawn from having a stand on solid ground, and there is no more solid and trustworthy place to stand on than the Word of God. This is the only true path anyone can follow. The reason is simple: Through Jesus, one is able to recognize and discard the negative, leaving the positive and bright side of life. Actually, I hoped that my sons observed the instances when I needed to "lift up" some friends or acquaintances. This was necessary when they began to express pity because of my inability to see. I make sure that I quickly correct this negative perception. In some cases, physical blindness is less debilitating than spiritual blindness. I am about to say something that would cause some to wonder about the state of my sanity—I would affirm that sight is a sense that, in some instances, can be done away with. Why would I say such a thing? Because having physical sight may cause one to rely on what is seen rather than trust in our God, whom we cannot physically see—this can result in a more destructive spiritual handicap!

It was important to me that my sons learn what to do in all circumstances, not because of what I taught them but because what God teaches. His instructions are detailed and include aspects of everything. His advice doesn't miss anything we may encounter. For example, in the area of maintaining optimism, our mind has to entertain positive and encouraging thoughts. Here is how He spells out this instruction: "Finally, brethren, whatsoever things are true, whatsoever things are honest, whatsoever things are just, whatsoever things are pure, whatsoever things are lovely, whatsoever things are of good report; if there be any virtue, and if there be any praise, think on these things" (Philippians 4:8).

Overcoming Obstacles

As soon as our sons were old enough, we began teaching them about handling obstacles. Life is not about what you *cannot* do because of a circumstance out of your control. Success comes when you recognize what you *can* do because of what God has given you. I wanted them to be aware that when they act alone, their own resources are limited. Those resources, however, have no limit when they turn to God, who can help them to overcome any obstacles they would undoubtedly face. I desired to teach them the value of God's Word as a point of reference when they formed their values. This was important as they recognized and discerned the destructive effect of the greatest obstacle of all—sin. Removing this obstacle can only be done with Christ's wisdom. Only then, will they be able to recognize the pitfalls created by this world's deceptive values. It will also be through the wisdom obtained from God that they will learn of the freedom found by following His Word.

Much Needed Darkness

Elevators and our lives are very similar. You might be thinking, "What a strange comparison!" But did you ever see an elevator go up or down while the door is still opened? Of course not, the door must be closed before it can move. Once the door is closed, however, it would be pitch dark inside it if it weren't for the light purposely installed.

Sometimes, it's also necessary to experience some closed doors in our lives, the darkness of trials, losses, setbacks. I believe that my sons could easily remain stuck, stagnant, and unable to move forward and grow to become stronger unless some door closes, creating a certain degree of darkness. It is this darkness that might be necessary in order for the light of the Word of God to hold more value, similar to the elevator, which does not move until that door is closed. It's this darkness that brings forth the depth and value found in the powerful light of the Word of God. In order for my sons to grow closer and have a deeper relationship with Jesus, they might need to experience some darkness in order for His light to shine brighter. Is darkness in a life always necessary to see God's light? Perhaps not, but I find that the deeper the valley, the greater the glory as His hand lifts you to the top of the mountain!

Every parent wants his or her children to be safe, including me, safe from all harm, pain, or suffering. Safety, however, is not the absence of storms, but the presence of Jesus. At the risk of sounding strange, I'd like to share with you that making my sons "happy" is not a priority for me. Sheltering them from difficulties for the sake of making them happy may be counterproductive. I find that if my sons are kept from experiencing some difficulties and hardships in life, they will not grow emotionally or spiritually. Teaching them the path to follow in situations of painful adversity is what will hold lasting value for them.

I tried to show them that trials in life are simply tests. These tests, however, are different from those they took in school. No grade is given. Adversity and pain in this life are these tests…they are the open-book type of tests. The book is the Bible. If you make the effort, it's impossible to fail—the answers are all clearly given in its pages!

Sin Is Sin

Our house in Florida includes a nice size pool, surrounded by palm trees, flowers, and bushes in a variety of colors. I enjoy soaking up some sun by the pool whenever I have time. But what I very seldom do is get in the pool. During the years we lived in this house, I have gone in the water only a half dozen times. Those of you reading this who enjoy swimming pools are most probably saying, what a fool! I guess my answer to that would be that there is something about soaking in chlorine that simply doesn't excite me.

There is one member of our family, however, who thoroughly enjoys this feature of our home. My Dad would get in that pool any time of the year, hot, cold, cloudy, or sunny...it wouldn't matter. One day in December, I asked him with astonishment, how could he possibly stand that cold water! His response was, "It's cold at first, but then you get used to it and it's just fine and enjoyable."

WOW! Regarding sin...that is exactly what I didn't want my sons to say! I didn't just want them to be initially shocked at sin, immorality, or destructive behavior. I also hoped that they would not begin to accept it by growing accustomed to it! I wanted them to see what is wrong is always wrong. When you disobey God, there are consequences. Unlike getting adjusted to the temperature of the water in the swimming pool, they needed to know the danger of "getting used to" behavior that is accepted by society but offensive to God!

The Shield of Protection

There is something very strange about the swimming pools in Florida. At least it seemed strange to me when I first moved here. I had never seen this before. I'm referring to the large screen that encloses the whole pool, even the tall palm trees. When this enclosure was first described to me, I pictured it as a huge birdcage...and there we were on our patio chairs, looking like birds sitting on their perches inside it. "How silly," I thought. But one evening when we had friends visiting us, we sat outside. The weather was so delightful, but there was something else that we enjoyed. While protected inside the huge screen, no bugs or insects of any kind ever bothered us!

This reminded me of the job I had to do for my sons as well. I had to make sure that our sons understood that God's Word had not been spoken with the purpose of binding us, limiting us, or confining us like a cage. Rather, similar to the screen around our swimming pool, it provides them with protection, a protection that keeps them from going down destructive paths.

Being Productive

I have always tried to pass on to my sons the lessons that I have learned myself. For example, I am the most comfortable when I'm in the process of multi-tasking. I try to do this any chance I get. I know that I only have four senses left. No, I shouldn't say "only" four. Actually, four is pretty good especially when I make up for the sense of sight by "thinking." Yes, I try to use that portion of my brain that is otherwise "idle" because it's not receiving any signals from my retina. I figured, no sense in wasting that part of the brain, wouldn't you agree? So I need to put it to good use. I love to think, ponder, and reflect. I take in the sound teachings of Scripture, as well as create material to teach and even write. I write letters to my sons; some I mail to them, some I email, and some I have even left on their pillows. I like to share with them concepts, advice, instructions, warnings, and praise for what they've done.

I like to keep my brain occupied all the time. I guess that for this reason, sitting in front of the TV is one thing I detest. It's not what you're thinking—that I can't see the screen. No, not at all; I know what's going on because I can hear the nonsense coming through the tube just fine. I like to impart this insight to my sons as well. For that reason, when I see them in front of it, I remind them (OK, I admit it...I nag), constantly that they should be productive as much as possible. I suggest they wait until they're at least ninety-nine years old, when their bodies may not be as responsive, to sit before the mindless tyrant (TV) and have the leisure of exercising only their thumb as they operate the remote control. Sometimes they even listen to their mom.

Good vs. Evil

I began to instill biblical principles in the boys when they were very young. Bedtime was usually my time to do this. Rather than just discuss sports or school issues, I would teach them Bible verses. In the similar way in which I taught them to have a good sense of humor, I also wanted to teach them as many godly concepts as I could. My hope was that they would apply all of it to their lives as they grew up. I related to them the importance of recognizing the battle we face between good and evil. The forces that cause us to fall are strong and therefore a complete protection is needed. I taught them that spiritual protection is provided specifically from God. I shared with them that the only way to make sure that we're protected from the enemy was to put on the armor of God (Ephesians 6:10-18). The idea of putting on armor and all its components was something they could understand. They willingly repeated the passage with me until they had memorized it.

This type of spiritual battle might not have been a clear concept for them at their young age, but they would remember these verses now that they have grown up, and this battle between good and evil has become more relevant in their lives. Unfortunately, along with the rest of the world, they witnessed this terrifying fact of life through the events of the 9-11 tragedy. The evident way in which the battle of good and evil played out before our very eyes was difficult to miss. One specific instance was played out on Flight 93 of United Airlines. Two men ended their days on earth driven by different motives. The terrorist, who was motivated by hatred, sought vengeance to please his god. The other, a Christian passenger displaying faith in the God of the Bible, was motivated by love and courage to seek ways to save lives.

Why Fear?

Another lesson I hope to pass on to my sons was the importance of learning to recognize and acknowledge your emotions. I told them that the emotions such as anger, fear, anxiety, insecurity, etc., are part of being human. God created us with the ability to experience them from time to time. Jesus felt some of these emotions himself when He was on earth in human flesh. The most important thing to remember is that these emotions have a place, not in your heart but in Christ's hands. How to go about doing this? First by recognizing them for what they are. You cannot let go of something until you have identified it, acknowledged it, and recognized it for what it is. Then you can take that most important step...release it to Jesus. Why? Because His word instructs us to do so: "Casting all your care upon him, for he cares for you" (1 Peter 5:7).

I have told them that when they feel negative emotions, such as insecurity, jealousy, anxiety, or anger, they need to look at the reason behind it. When they do, they will always find that fear is at the root of it all. There are not too many negative emotions that don't originate with some type of fear, and here is God's insight on that: "There is no fear in love; but perfect love. But perfect love drives out fear, because fear has to do with punishment. The one who fears is not made perfect in love" (1 John 4:18). Love is the antidote for fear. Jesus is nothing less than perfect love.

Credit

"Be careful with the use of credit cards," I warn my sons over and over again...but that's just me talking. Does God's

Word address this issue? Does it give insight about the danger of "borrowing" on credit cards? Among the many warnings and instructions He gives, here is one, "Just as the rich rule the poor, so the borrower is a servant to the lender" (Proverbs 22:7 NLT).

Listen to the Coach

As I mentioned to you before, I like to write letters to my sons. Through the years, I must have written dozens and dozens to them. Most letters are short and to the point. They address any current issues going on at that particular time in their lives. I'd like to share with you a letter I wrote to our son Jeff. He was struggling to make a final decision regarding his major in college.

May 20, 2003

Dear Jeff:

Do you remember when you were in your senior year at Cypress Creek High School and you received the MVP award at the lacrosse banquet? What a great time that was for you, for Dad and your brothers, as well as for me! I guess you can attribute this success to your dedication and your hard work, not to forget the skill and ability God has given you. If you were to think about what took place through the four years of playing this sport, I'm sure that you will agree that you had some pretty good coaches. Mr. Sloop was a great coach. He was the one who gave you the instructions as you first began to play that sport. You were smart, you listened to him attentively. You needed to listen because you had not held a lacrosse stick before! Slowly, you began to trust in Mr. Sloop's coaching abilities—his insight, his knowledge, as well as his caring nature for you and the team. You obeyed his instructions; you followed the tips he gave with diligence. He led you and the team to many victories...he knew the path!

While Dad and I watched (actually I attended and listened), Dad was the one who watched attentively each of your games. I loved to hear your name over the loudspeaker: "One more goal for Cypress Creek by number 34, Jeff Eckles!" Since I couldn't see the game, those announcements were extra special to me. You were doing exactly what coach had instructed you to do. You reached the goals. You even went beyond...remember how often you were the highest scorer?

Life is no different, Jeff; you have the best coach of life. Jesus is the one who knows the perfect path that will lead you to victory. He is your coach, giving you detailed directions that you need to follow. He will show the moves you need to make when you seek the right major in college, the right job, and the correct way to perform a task. He is your coach who wants nothing more than to see you succeed. His plan for your life doesn't include just career success, but much, much more. Looking to Him will guarantee victory in the all-star game of life!

While playing lacrosse, you would never think of ignoring Mr. Sloop's instructions...he knew more than you. Neither you nor the team would think of attempting to play a game without his leadership and guidance. In the same manner, Jeff, my prayer is that you not ignore Jesus; instead, seek His wisdom. Life will flow much better for you as you follow His leadership and guidance—they are spelled out for you in the Bible. He has the perfect plan for your life...commit to follow it!

From the moment you wake up, seek his Word. He will reveal what you need to do. He will keep you from going down paths leading nowhere. He will guard your steps. Going about life without Jesus is like learning to play a sport without a coach. Unprepared to play the game, you're bound to lose.

Just like you needed diligence and dedication to play lacrosse, in order to follow Jesus, you need the same diligence and commitment to His Word. Practice is held daily, the instruction book is the Bible, the equipment is your discipline, no need to keep score...victory is guaranteed! And don't forget your cheerleader—me.

I love you,

Mom

27

Religion vs. Relationship

"I'm not as religious as you are, Jan," a friend informed me some time ago. Hmmm...what does that mean...religious? If it means that my life is centered on my Lord Jesus Christ, that He is my focus, my all...if it means that my heart is aligned with His so I wouldn't depart from Him...if it means that my desire is to align my values with His Word...if that is what "religious" means, then "religious" is my middle name!

"How do you know that I have been sitting at my desk for hours?" I asked Dr. Ben, while lying face down on the adjustment table. "Because I'm your chiropractor and I know your back" was his reply. Dr. Ben happens to be one of the most respected chiropractors in the country. I admire him not because he is a much sought-after chiropractor but because he is a godly man, one who makes no attempt to hide his faith in Christ. His wisdom is drawn from God. For that reason, his insights and teachings about fitness, nutrition, stress, and health, such as the ones he describes in his bestseller, *Body by God,* are those that I rely on. I try to follow his suggestions from his God-given knowledge. This has kept me healthier than I have ever been. Except for a minor cold every few years, my health and level of energy are blessings I enjoy with gratitude.

One of the things that Dr. Ben has passed on to me is that the alignment of the spinal cord is crucial to the overall health of a person. The misalignment of the spinal cord can result in other parts of the body, including the vital organs, to perform with deficiency. So what does this have to do with religion versus relationship? It's very simple. Here is the conclusion according to Jan: With religion, your mind receives doctrine after doctrine but if your heart is not aligned with Christ's, then there is no personal connection with him. And just like a misaligned back, other areas of your life don't work well.

Relationship with Jesus on the other hand is quite different. Your heart is aligned with Him. There is a perfect connection. Your thoughts and His words are in perfect line with each other. With this alignment, all areas of your life work perfectly.

What happens when disease comes along to a person with a misaligned spinal cord? Healing is difficult because areas of the body, such as the immune system, are not working at their optimum. Similarly, when adversity enters a person focused on religion only, healing is also difficult because there is no relationship with Jesus.

What happens when adversity enters into a life that is aligned with Christ? Healing takes place much easier because the connection with Jesus, the Divine Healer, has already been established. Healing occurs by drawing from His wisdom and sustaining power.

I've heard many say, "I don't believe in organized religion." I don't blame them—organized or unorganized religion, when lacking a complete relationship with Jesus, has no meaning or substance. It would be like planning a fancy dinner party. Everything is carefully arranged; the decorations are put in place. The guests arrive…but there is no food!

If you would allow me to expand the difference between the two R's a little further, here is how the Webster's Seventh Collegiate Dictionary defines the two words:

Religion: Commitment or devotion to religious faith or observance system of religious attitudes, beliefs, and practices. *Relationship:* The state of character of being related or interrelated.

More important than the definitions, however, is the enormous significance this distinction has made in my life. It wasn't the religion but the relationship with Jesus that brought me from the darkness of sorrow to the light of His Word.

Building a Relationship

Building a meaningful relationship takes time as well as willingness and determination. I had all of the above when it came to Gene. I knew about him, a friend told me who he was. We met, were attracted to one another. We began to spend time together. Sharing each moment drew us closer and closer. We made the decision to spend the rest of our lives together. Through the years, I feel that I know him so well that often I can predict his reaction to any particular situation. I can even tell by the way he clears his throat what the tone will be as he speaks. I know him intimately.

It was no different with Jesus. I knew about Him. I was attracted by His loving nature. I began to spend time with Him. Through the written Word in the Bible, I observed His reactions toward the woman at the well, His compassion toward the thief on the cross next to Him, His anger towards the merchants who defiled God's house, His teachings about pride, hypocrisy, gossip, etc. I saw His tenderness toward the adulteress; His loving promises to those who suffer. I noted how He answered my every prayer. I chose to make Him my partner for life.

I developed an intimate relationship with Gene and with Jesus. Here is the difference: I'm certain that Gene would be willing to do anything for me; on the other hand, Jesus already did everything for me. He accomplished everything by dying on the cross and bringing me from darkness to light, finally leading me by the hand through the most excruciating and agonizing episode of losing our son Joe.

28

Guarding the Mind

C an I ask your assistance for a moment? Would you be so kind as to press the "rewind" button? Rewind my story back to the part when I had to turn in my car keys because my vision had deteriorated so drastically.

Driving even in familiar places became a physical and emotional struggle for me, especially since my main goal was to get to our destination safely. I had to make sure that the conditions were favorable, meaning that my seven-, five-, and three-year-old sons had to cooperate in a big way. So I had a plan on how to achieve this. First I told the boys what they needed to do. I was firm with my instructions. Second, I told them how to do what I had asked. Finally, I would inform them of the reward they would receive when we got home.

The Lord also has a plan...a very specific one for each one of us. First, He gives clear instructions. Next, He tells us how to go about achieving them. Finally, He informs us of the rewards.

Walk with me through this process, which God outlines in Philippians 4:6-7. But before you do, would you make sure that you have in mind the burden your heart holds. I ask you this because when I was hurting and anxious, I obtained the answer through this promise. I knew that this passage was meant for me. I am convinced that God had you in mind as well. Obeying these steps will guarantee peace...one that goes beyond all understanding.

This is His clear instruction: "Be anxious for nothing..." (Philippians 4:6).

Here He tells us how to achieve this: "but in everything by prayer and supplication, with thanksgiving, let your requests be made known to God" (v. 6).

Here is what we can expect from a trustworthy God: "And the peace of God, which surpasses all understanding, will guard your hearts and minds through Christ Jesus" (v. 7 NKJV).

But why would our minds need guarding? Because the thoughts that the mind entertains will dictate how the emotions play out. Holding positive and reassuring thoughts is a simple task in ideal circumstances. In the middle of a crisis, however, that's a different story. For this reason, the Bible says that the guarding of our minds will be done not on our own, but "through Christ Jesus." It is precisely through Him that we can have the confidence to conquer the onset of potentially debilitating thoughts. God, our creator, knows full well how vulnerable our minds can be. This vulnerability is particularly evident at night, as the darkness and silence create an ideal playground for the enemy and his attacks. So where do we find the comforting and trustworthy solution for this? What will be our shield against this?

"He will shield you with his wings! They will shelter you. His faithful promises are your armor. Now you don't need to be afraid of the dark any more, nor fear the dangers of the day; nor dread the plagues of darkness, nor disasters in the morning" (Psalm 91:4-6 TLB).

Allowing God's Word to fill my mind gives me clarity to put everything into perspective. This includes the memories my heart holds. For instance, Joe was not the most obedient young man, but there was one area where he would always obey me without exception. This was when I asked him to pray with me. He would immediately drop anything he was doing, and we would hold hands and pray. This is a memory that brings more than just warm thoughts of my son.

Those of you who are parents will most probably identify with this. When it comes to our children, there are memories that are more than just pleasant thoughts. They are precious jewels wrapped in the soft velvet of tenderness, held together with gold strings of love. They are tucked in the most inner depth of your heart. One such memory I have of my Joe took place right after he received Jesus into his heart.

As was typical of Joe, when he had something important to discuss with Gene and me, he would burst into our room. This particular instance, he was seventeen years old and had just come back from the Fellowship of Christian Athletes (FCA) camp (see chapter 17). He said, with insistence, "Guys, we have to pray." We were very aware that he had just given his young life to the Lord. Without hesitation Gene and I agreed. The words, intonation, and conviction with which Joe prayed then now echo in my mind as if it happened moments ago. He prayed, "Thank you, Jesus, for coming into my life, thank you for giving me parents who support me and are willing to pray with me. Thank you for everything you have done for me." When I see Joe the next time—not if, but when—I will say to him, "Thank you, son, for giving me the greatest gift a Mom could receive!"

Facing Reality

It's also important for Jesus to guard our minds in order to face reality. This is crucial when the reality is painful. This certainly was the case as we lived through the death of our Joe.

Yet the truth is that Joe is more alive than any one of us. He did not put off his salvation by thinking that there is always a tomorrow to seek it. His life brought to reality what the Bible says regarding our days on earth, "Whereas you do not know what will happen tomorrow. For what is your life? It is even a vapor that appears for a little time and then vanishes away" (James 4:14 NKJV).

It is also a reality that Joe's life on earth was brief, but not without a purpose.

I was delighted beyond words when Joe had given his life to Christ two years before his physical death. But giving his heart to Christ as Joe did in his short life had to mean more than just making this decision. It meant that he had to stay unashamedly committed to Jesus. In his own way, he demonstrated this conviction. A few short weeks before God called Joe home, he had a tattoo placed on his left arm. It was of a beautiful cross. Although Joe had always complied with our wishes not to have any tattoos on his body, only Joe and God know the real reason for him to make that decision at this particular time. He had intricately designed this cross;

it was not just any cross but one that held a special meaning for him and, later on, a special meaning for Gene and me.

A couple of weeks later, he and a group of childhood friends who were visiting Florida went to the beach. When he was asked the reason for the cross on his arm, he replied that he had accepted Christ as his Savior and this cross was a symbol of that commitment. Perhaps this was the last audible message Joe gave to his friends. But now this message from Joe speaks even louder to urge his friends to obtain their salvation.

As I mentioned before, God's promises often go even beyond what we expect.

Shortly after their brother began his life in heaven, Jason and Jeff gave their lives to Christ. As a sign of their commitment, they also chose to have the same cross placed on their arms. More importantly, they placed Jesus in their hearts. Although they will have to face many tests and perhaps struggle in their walk with Jesus, I feel peace in knowing that they will not go through life aimlessly looking for a purpose, for the only way for them to find true purpose is by answering Jesus' call to follow Him.

29

Getting Over It

❧

All of us, at one time or another, experience the loss of something or someone important to us. In my case, the loss of sight and the loss of Joe marked painful episodes in my journey. The stages of the grieving process are different for each person. I think that it is perfectly natural to shed tears when faced with a tragedy of this magnitude. Gene and I have allowed ourselves to have what we call "sobbing moments." They are just that: sporadic moments. However, they don't turn into days. The only reason we are able to move on is because we didn't face this alone. Jesus is the one who kept us from being paralyzed by this emotion. Gene and I have encouraged Joe's brothers not to keep inside the feelings their hearts may hold. I also feel that it is important for me not to "cover up" the moments of grief and tears. Taking medication to ease the pain could perhaps cause me to rely on its effects rather than on the Words of God that echo in my heart: "It shall come to pass in the day the LORD gives you rest from your sorrow, and from your fear and the hard bondage in which you were made to serve" (Isaiah 14:3). Also, "Fear not, for I am with you; be not dismayed, for I am your God. I will strengthen you, Yes, I will help you, and I will uphold you with my righteous right hand" (Isaiah 41:10).

These are the promises that soothed my heart and thus became the prescription that provided the best medicine for my soul. God's endless love for us was portrayed not only through these promises but also through our family, friends, and our church. The support and genuine care they displayed overwhelmed us and turned our moments of confusion and sadness into ones of extreme comfort. Now that our hearts held the certainty and reassurance that Joe is in the glory of his permanent home, our lives needed to move forward.

But how do you begin to do that after such a loss? What happens when everyone else goes home to his or her unchanged lives and our days begin the difficult attempt to go back to our "normal" routine? To make this process easier, Gene and I thought that it would be helpful to talk to other parents who might have experienced a similar loss. We looked and looked for a parent's group based on biblical principles. We were unsuccessful. We decided to attend a secular support group in our area. God was at work here as well in a powerful way. He used this experience to reinforce the need to have Him in our lives. It was as if He was saying to us, "You'll see…I have the answer when others don't."

We didn't know what to expect from this group. Although the leaders were very supportive and understanding, we found nothing new or revealing. We realized that a group would not be beneficial to us if it excluded a focus on Jesus.

The one aspect that negatively impressed me about this group was the deep sorrow and lack of peace, which some parents still displayed even when it had been years since their loss. A lady who was sitting in front of us shared with Gene and me the circumstances of the loss of her son. Through her tears and with a trembling voice, she related that she still felt an intense anger over her son's loss. This tragic event had taken place one year ago. She added that she had not gone through one day without crying for her child. My heart was so moved with compassion. As Gene and I attempted to console her, every fiber of my being wanted to share with her the peace and sustaining power obtained through Jesus.

During that single two-hour session, we heard bits of stories shared by parents who were tangibly drowning in inconsolable sorrow. My heart was torn and I wished that I had a magic wand to ease their pain. I also couldn't help but wonder... "How do you get over a tragedy such as this one?" Do you ever, in fact, "get over" losing a child? Do you get over any tragedy that impacts your life beyond words? I believe that the resounding and emphatic answer is "No." I think that doing so implies that you would dismiss it, deny it, forget it, or pretend it didn't happen. You don't get over it; instead, you let Jesus take over. Although I reference this concept by relating it in a more trivial way, it may help to illustrate the point.

Gene and I are often as amazed at Jason's incredible artistic gift of drawing as we are Jeff and Joe's natural ability to excel at any sport they played. We are amazed not so much for the talent but its origin. We ask ourselves, which one of us did they get it from? Neither one of us has artistic abilities or sport abilities. As a matter of fact, I remember the one solitary sport I attempted to participate in was very short-lived. In my freshman year of high school, I decided to give sports a try by joining the track team. The event most suitable for me was the relay races. It seemed easy enough because I knew that I didn't have to run the whole race. I was only responsible for the portion that brought me to the next person who would receive the baton. I remember that in the two or maybe three races I participated in, I felt extreme relief when I finally handed the baton to that next runner. I was off the hook, I had done my part, I didn't need to be concerned about the end of the race, and I could rest knowing that someone else had taken over.

In my own emotional race, I had to let Jesus take over as well. Rather than try to run while holding on to the burden of my heart-wrenching anguish, an emotion so intense that it could take my breath away and paralyzes my life, if I would hand it to Him, He would take over, allowing me to rest. He promised, "Come to me, all you who labor and are heavy laden, and I will give you rest. Take My yoke upon you and learn from Me, for I am gentle and lowly in heart, and you will find rest for your souls. For My yoke is easy and My burden is light" (Matthew 11:28-30 NKJV).

My heart is relieved when I know that Jesus' invitation is directed to me, so that I can freely come to Him and know that I don't have to run the painful race of life alone. When I obey His word, He is ready to take over by fulfilling His promises, the same ones that had sustained me through times of trouble over and over again.

30

My Cross

I wonder if, while reading my story, you have thought about your own cross. Let me reassure you that all of us have crosses to carry in this less-than-perfect world. The degree to which this burden affects a life depends on where the focus is placed.

Every chance we get, Gene and I take time to enjoy one of our favorite activities. We take the one-hour trip to Cocoa Beach from our home in Orlando. We relax and rest by enjoying the ocean, the soft beaches, and the warm sun. Once we have spent a few hours relaxing and resting, it's time to go home. We pack our things and begin our walk back to the car. While Gene carries all the heavier items, I carry my beach bag full of the necessary things. I admit I probably take more than I really need. As a result, this bag tends to be somewhat heavy. I hold it with one arm while I use the other to hold on to Gene. This walk back to our car is not pleasant. My bag becomes awkward to carry as my feet sink into the soft sand. Each step causes me to lose my balance as I try to keep the bag in place, my sandals from slipping off, and my hat from flying into the wind. As my bag seems to get heavier with each uncomfortable step, I ask Gene, with a somewhat impatient tone, how close we are to the boardwalk. His response is always the same, "Pretty close."

Once this painful walk, which seems to take forever, ends at the boardwalk, things change. It then becomes much easier to carry the bag. I now have a sure footing on a solid and firm surface. Not only that, but I have a new focus, which is on the car located nearby in the parking lot. Now I can be confident that we'll soon be rid of the items we carry and will be on our way home. Although the weight of the bag didn't change, my focus did, making the bag seem lighter and much easier to carry.

The pain I hold on to because of what happened to our Joe is quite similar to the heavy bag. When I stand and dwell on its devastating effect, it can be overwhelming and unbearable. I'm then sure to lose my balance and be tempted to give up. Giving up would allow the pain to sink me into the sand of sorrow. But when I choose to stand on the solid and trustworthy foundation provided by the Word of God, I can move ahead through life. My steps become secure and confident. My focus is no longer on me or on my pain but on Jesus' promises. They provide me with the lasting security I need. My focus on Him alone allows the pain of Joe's absence to be a tender reminder of just how much I love Joe. It's no longer a debilitating burden.

My desire is not to over-simplify this difficult process of dealing with intense pain, so I would like to expand on the steps I took and the revelations I found as I moved from the stage of grief to one of peace and reassurance, which starts with a passage from Matthew: "Then Jesus said to his disciples, 'If anyone desires to come after me, let him deny himself, and take up his cross, and follow me'" (Matthew 16:24).

So what does this passage really mean in terms of dealing with grief? It's simple for anyone, referring to Bible verses, to write down concepts and ideas that seem logical and comforting. It's something completely different to put into practice an instruction such as the above verse.

First of all, what does it mean to "follow Him?" I imagine that I'm an authority when it comes to following. Every time I go out anywhere, I'm holding on to someone's arm, following as he or she leads me...simple task for me! The reason it's simple is because I happen to trust the person, but more importantly, I know with certainty where they're leading me.

It became just as simple to follow Jesus...I knew without a doubt where He was leading me to—to peace, reassurance, security, and strength.

I take physical steps when I follow as I hold on to someone's arm; I take spiritual steps holding on to Jesus. The steps to follow are the ones found in every verse of every passage in the Bible. They come alive impacting my heart outlining the path.

I don't know about you, but I always want to be *shown* how to do something. Concepts and their explanations simply don't hit home with me. So let me illustrate what I mean when I say that I had to "follow Jesus."

Not long ago, a few couples, including Gene and I, decided to go to play putt-putt golf. I very seldom will say, "I can't do that," just because I can't see. On the contrary, I love to try new things and, of course, I have to learn how to do them without sight. With the golf, Gene's patience once again was at work. He stood behind me and gently showed me how to hold the club properly.

"This is so that the ball will go where you want it to," he said. He showed me how to align my feet, how far to put them apart, and how to align my shoulders correctly. I followed these instructions diligently, at least for the first few holes. Then, I thought, "What difference does it make how I stand, or how to hold the club After all it wasn't a comfortable position and I wanted to do it my way by standing the way I was accustomed to. Not only that, eighteen holes is just too much and too long for me to continue to do it 'his' way."

How similar this was to when I first followed Jesus. He gives specific instructions about every possible circumstance one could ever face. It's easy at the beginning to look to His Word and follow it. It becomes much more difficult as crisis clouds our thinking. We tend to go back to our own way of rationalizing.

However, following Jesus means to consciously choose to look to see what He says and what He instructs. Where does He point me?

The answer is found in Hebrews 13:5: "Let your conduct be without covetousness; be content with such things as you have. For He Himself has said, 'I will never leave you nor forsake you.' So we may boldly say: 'The LORD is my helper; I will not fear' " (NKJV).

No matter how dreadful I think the circumstances will be, I can count on Jesus—I won't be alone. He promised that He would never abandon me, and I believe Him. Knowing that this is a trustworthy promise, I have a renewed sense of confidence, peace comes back, and each day is lived to its fullest.

That's what it means to follow Jesus, but what about the cross? Depending on the circumstances, the "cross" may represent a heart filled with sadness, pain, loneliness, anguish, or desperation. All these could be called spiritual ailments. Similar to a family doctor that often heals the illness, Jesus is the one to provide the complete healing. Actually He is the perfect healer, specializing in heart problems, ones that affect the emotional and spiritual stability. We head to the doctor with our diseases; similarly we should follow the path to Jesus with our cross.

It's important to know whom we're following, how we choose to follow, but it's also essential to know *why* we're following. The reason to follow Jesus with our cross, whatever that might be, is because there will be a point of exchange...we'll exchange our cross for His grace. Why His grace? Because that is the power, although inexplicable, is ever present and available to all. Figuring out how it works would be impossible...until one lives through it to experience it firsthand. Unable to see anything put in front of me, I sit before this computer sharing with you the joy, comfort, and hope my heart holds after a few months of losing my son—THAT'S GOD'S GRACE!

"...And he said unto me, My grace is sufficient for thee: for my strength is made perfect in weakness" (2 Corinthians 12:9).

Questions

Some would ask why do bad things happen to good people? I would ask instead why do *good* things happen to us? The goodness of God is that He chose not to be fair but to love. Had He been fair, we would all be condemned to eternal death because of our sins, but that is not the case. "For God so loved the world that He gave His only begotten Son, that whosoever believes in Him should not perish but have everlasting life" (John 3:16 NKJV).

While on this earth, sporadic pain and suffering for good or bad people is a given, but giving in is a choice. For me, there was only one choice, one option, one answer, one solution and one truth—Jesus.

But really, "Who do you think Jesus is?" This was a question Jesus himself asked one of his disciples. I wonder if I could be so intrusive as to ask you the same question. Who do you think that Jesus is? If your answer is that He is the only Savior, the Lord and God of all ages, the only truth, and on Him depends our salvation...and you would add that you know this because it was taught to you at a very young age, I would say that you have been blessed! As you know by reading the details of my life, it was different for me; I didn't grow up with this knowledge. I had to learn of His powerful love by going through trials. I guess you could say that I learned this the hard way. But it doesn't matter how I got to this point. The important thing is that I have come to know the life-giving source found in Jesus. I've come to know this truth after lessons learned first hand. I had to first be sightless before I could see Jesus. In order for me to appreciate the blood He shed for me, I had to first shed tears of my own pain. I had to first be broken before I could allow Him to make me whole. It wasn't until I lost a child that I could see firsthand God's victory over death.

Reflections on Life

I am resigned to and have accepted the fact that I now belonged to the group of parents who lost a child. At the same time, I inevitably came to reflect on my own life, my own mortality, my own specifically numbered days on this earth. I came to the conclusion that with Jesus, death is simply an acronym, one that should stand for:

Discarding
Erroneous
And
Terrifying
Half-truths.

Although we don't do this often enough, Gene and I enjoy taking the one and half-hour drive to visit his family in Daytona, Florida. The trip is not that long but we usually take some healthy snacks and plenty of water as well as a variety of topics to discuss in order to make the most of that time together. Often we take with us recorded Bible teachings, Christian programs, and other books on tape. Our listening material one hot spring day as we set off on one of these trips was *Tuesdays with Morrie* by Mitch Albom. With the humming of the engine in the background and the cooling comfort provided by the air conditioning, we both listened quietly as the author read the pages of this insightful book. Gene and I took in all the details of this story without making any comments. The book is about death and its preparation by a remarkable man as he faces this inevitable event. Since our Joe had just begun his new life with Christ, the end of this life on earth was fresh on our minds. Consequently, the issues expanded on in this story gave us reason to ponder and reflect, possibly with more depth than most. The book relates such a tender story that it's worth reading it twice. It is replete with powerful insights, philosophical observations, and valuable explanations regarding a variety of aspects of human life.

However, while I found that the book is full of great teachings presented in an easy-to-understand manner, I also realized it was empty of Jesus. Why would that be important? I think that if anyone would expand on the subject of death, Jesus, who is the one who conquered it, should be a crucial part of the story. Talking about the topic of death and disregarding Jesus is like writing the script for a western movie and excluding cowboys and horses.

I would like to offer my humble perception regarding the reality of physical death. I draw it from my own first hand experience of letting Joe go to be held by our creator's loving arms. I find that preparing for death as if death itself were the final end is similar to preparing for a long trip, packing the bags, buying the tickets, booking the tours, loading the car...only to make the airport the final destination. No one would do such a foolish thing. The airport should be the departing point, directing one to the most wonderful place to spend a vacation. Similarly for the believer, physical death is never the ultimate destination, but a departure point, one that begins the most glorious life of all! For those who don't know the salvation through Christ, then it would make sense if physical death would signify the end, with no hope, no mansion in which to reside in, no life to look forward to, no glory to see...nothing...just physical death leading to eternal death...but why would anyone in their right mind choose this if there is another option? Here it is: "And this is the record, that God hath given to us eternal life, and this life is in his Son. He that hath the Son hath life; and he that hath not the Son of God hath not life" (1 John 5:11-12).

I find it amazing and gratifying to know that any point mentioned in the Bible is often presented in many forms, in a variety of contexts, in several settings or circumstances—all have the same truth, the same message, the same clear point. The truth about eternal life is such an example: Jesus also said, "And whosoever lives and believes in me shall never die" (John 11:26).

These verses make it clear—the word "never" jumps out, emphasizing the point—that a life with Christ is a life full of hope that has no end; rather, it holds anticipation. Anticipating what we know for certain that awaits us! This is the reality! What is most exhilarating and absolutely wonderful is that God not only gives the final word about physical death but He provides the detailed and clear philosophies, advice, directions, and loving guidance regarding life. The life we live each day on this earth—He is a God about life, eternal life, not death! It's true that the days on this earth will end. No one can argue this. For some it may be sooner than others. But although this is an undeniable fact for all, for Christians death is not a cause for fear, or a subject to be silent about or dismiss and pretend it won't happen. On the contrary, believing in Jesus brings forth unequaled hope and encouragement spelled out in each promise from His Word. That is where the only security is found, one that cannot be provided by family members, friends, priests, pastors, rabbis, or teachers. Why not? Because this world is full of people who may have none of these—they may have no one at all! I personally have had the unfortunate experience of seeing people who latch on to comfort from this world. They desperately grab anything at all. They ultimately find the painful coldness as if they were holding a handful of ice cubes...melting quickly leaving them soaked in loneliness. I think Jesus knew this all too well because He offers the answer, "I will never leave you nor forsake you" (Hebrews 13:5 NKJV).

No one else can make this statement or fulfill it; nor can anyone give this level of reassurance. Jesus is present now, ready and able to provide all, absolutely all, that is needed. It is through Jesus that the essence and only worthwhile purpose of living on this earth is found. I think that one can live a hundred lifetimes and come up with a million philosophies and personal insights, yet only God's Word prevails, "For my thoughts are not your thoughts, nor are your ways my ways, says the LORD" (Isaiah 55:8).

Consequently, there are no other options that can be held up as being the absolute truth—His Word is final. Death is what He says it is, a bridge, not a bridge leading to the unknown, the abyss, or to a fearful darkness; but a necessary and short bridge to the life, the eternal life God created us to ultimately have!

Morrie and our Joe both had one thing in common; they both ended their days on this earth. One with a debilitating and terrible disease, Joe while he was at the peak of his health, energy, vitality, and youth. They both prepared for this inevitable step. Of course, Joe never anticipated the timing of his last breath, but he was prepared...by something that holds much more value. In fact there is no human value in this world's standards that could be placed for this gift... he chose to receive it and obtain his salvation. He chose eternal life!

Knowing this fact about Joe brought to light one of the sad ironies of life: Some men are forced to die trapped in a withering body, while others choose to live in an already withered soul!

Do you recall at the beginning of my story when I related to you how desperately I wished to have one more second of sight? God did not grant me that second; instead, He granted me a lifetime of spiritual sight to see His truth. The truth that is simple to see. It is not theologically complicated; it has no deep philosophy to ponder upon, no complex insight to digest. It is just a simple truth, the one that rings loudly, even as the values blurred out by men through the centuries lose their meaning by vanishing into thin air. What is left behind, always is one clear, solid, and everlasting fact—with Jesus, physical death is not the end but the beginning!

31

Moving On

Now that we can put aside any feelings of fear regarding death, there is more energy left to jump the hurdles that are part of this running track we call life. With Christ as the coach, our job is to follow His instructions in order to put our life "together" again. However, this is not an easy task particularly after suffering a crisis.

I have a godly friend named Sandy. We met as she came to my door one day. Since she is a neighbor, she wanted to see if there was anything she could do for me at the time I was grieving for Joe. We began to talk and share where our hearts were in relation to Christ. In doing so, we learned that we had much in common. Just like me, she had a desire to pray for our neighbors and attempt to bring God's truth to them. We began to walk and pray. We organized some events for a few of the ladies. Several responded, and now we have a great group of ladies where we discuss issues of life and find solutions based on the Bible.

One day, Sandy related to me that while she was walking in a crowded parking lot, she stopped as she noticed an older lady carrying her grandbaby in her arms, struggling to assemble a stroller. This is a difficult task if only one hand is free. Sandy, as is her caring nature, quickly approached her and offered her help. She knew her limitations when it comes to "assembling" things so she did the next best thing. "I'd be happy to hold the baby so that you can have free hands to assemble it," she offered. The lady readily accepted Sandy's kind gesture. While Sandy held the baby, this grateful grandmother removed latches, adjusted and put things in place, and it was now ready for the baby. Sandy handed the little bundle back, exchanged some polite phrases, and they all continued their separate ways.

"Sandy!" I exclaimed. "That is exactly what God did in my life." I couldn't assemble my life together because I was holding to that "something," which often gets in the way. It keeps you in a struggling mode, unable to put your life together again. But the minute Jesus said, "I will take it from you. Cast that burden onto me," then I was free. Under His watchful eye, I began to reassemble my life once again.

Bumps in the Road

As I push my newly assembled life forward, the surface is not always smooth. There are still bumps that get in the way and force me to stop abruptly. That is when I turn to Jesus…just to make sure that I'm not alone. He always reassures me as He guides me to a detour He has prepared for me. This way the path is free, allowing my life to move forward once again.

When I listen to the contents of what I wrote in Chapter 20, my heart skips a beat, my fingers slow down, and they seem to be unable to move through the keyboard. I hit a bump, a painful bump. It's because the details of that night still present an emotional bump for me.

I have a dear friend named Chris. We have been friends for many years. Although we now live miles from one another, she often shows her love in very sweet ways. From time to time, she says to me, with a soft and caring voice, "Got something for you!" I know exactly what she means. She must have found a garment at a bargain price. Given the limited time I have to shop for clothes, I am always so appreciative of this kind gesture on her part. Whatever Chris buys fits me like a glove. She knows my size, my taste, and the colors I can wear, as well as the style I like.

And, as a close friend, Chris knows just what I need when it comes to clothing. Similarly Jesus, as my Lord and Savior, knows my heart. He knows exactly what I need now and what I will need in my days to come. When those painful bumps appear as the different stages of the court proceedings take place, He will undoubtedly provide me with exactly what I need, the strength, the peace, the wisdom, and reassurance.

How do I know for sure? To answer this question, I will test your memory. As you began to read my story, do you remember how Jesus alone brought me out of my desperation while my sight was closing in? Do you remember how He sustained me through the moments when I learned of what happened to our Joe? If you do, I'm sure that you'll agree that He'll also be by my side as I face the moments ahead.

32

Becoming Wiser

I've become wiser; wise enough to recognize the immense value of God's protection. Also wise enough to find new reasons to be grateful.

His Protection

"What do you mean it's not covered!" I responded with surprise and frustration. I was on the phone with a health insurance representative, discussing a bill from a medical facility. The charges were for a routine test for Gene. Having a great deal of experience of dealing with insurance companies, I had taken all the steps to make sure that this procedure would be covered at the highest level of benefits. I checked to see if the doctor and the facility were both within the network. I also verified to make sure that there was no need for pre-authorization of any kind, etc. Feeling very confident with my adequate research, Gene had completed the procedure with no problem. But this is when I came to learn that it wasn't covered after all. The reason given was that this procedure was "routine."

"Ma'am, it would have been covered 100 percent if your husband had any ailments. Sorry, but this procedure is considered routine in his case. Only minimal coverage can be extended under your plan," explained the insurance representative.

Guilty! I admit…I didn't read the small print in the policy! (Or should I say, I didn't ask Gene to read it.) Small print or not, it's a fact of life that health, car, and life insurance protection is necessary for all.

I know all about protection. One of the advantages of living in the sunshine state is that the weather allows us to take long walks any time of the year. Gene and I try to do this as often as we can. He takes my hand, and we begin to follow the usual path around our neighborhood. After almost twenty-five years of leading me, he has developed a very effective way to swiftly guide me around any obstacle, up or down any step or sidewalk. I can easily follow his hand as he leads me through any narrow path or uneven spots.

Our walks are usually uneventful and enjoyable, but on one occasion we were suddenly met with the loud barking of two large dogs. To my surprise, they were not behind a fence, which is usually the case whenever we hear barking. These dogs charged us, barking furiously. We stopped and Gene quickly put me behind him, providing a shield of protection. (I've never been more appreciative of the fact that Gene is twice as big as I am!) They continued to bark and growl as they came closer and closer. Even when they began to jump on him, Gene somehow took care of the situation. I was somewhat shaken, but I felt protected and secure. Eventually, the owners came and retrieved them and we continued on.

Gene was able to lead me behind him easily and quickly because I was already holding on to his hand. I have also made it a practice to hold on to Jesus in my walk through life. I hold on to Him for protection because He is my insurance against any perils that may come along. Being separated from

His love would be like canceling all insurance policies. The best policy of protection is His endless love. It provides coverage against all. This policy has no exclusion, no disclaimers, no expiration date, and no small print. It reads in bold letters the following reassurances: "Who shall separate us from the love of Christ? Shall tribulation, or distress, or persecution, or famine, or nakedness, or peril, or sword?" (Romans 8:35 NKJV). "Nor height, nor depth, nor any other created thing, shall be able to separate us from the love of God, which is in Christ Jesus our Lord" (Romans 8:39 NKJV).

Along with the walks Gene and I take, we also like to get some exercise by an occasional bike ride. Yes, those tandem bikes come in handy. We pedal through our neighborhood, enjoying the cool breeze and the fragrance of the flowers coming from our neighbor's gardens. My job is easy; I just pedal. I'm not concerned with anything else. Gene has full control. He knows the path to take, and he is the one to look for cars as we cross the streets. He can see ahead for any uneven spots or any obstacles we need to avoid. Given my inability to see, there is no other option but for Gene to be in the front seat and me in the back.

It's no different when I place myself behind the secure protection of God's Word. Jesus who can see my days ahead goes before me. There is no other option—I put myself behind Him with confidence.

My Gratitude

"Go to your room!" was my usual way to solve a situation when the boys were younger and had really tested my patience to the limit. But this particular time, one of them had done something that required, in my opinion, a lecture to make him understand why he was being punished. However, an upset Mom and an angry child are not the best combination. It's wise to let things cool off before attempting to reason out the problem.

I decided to write him a note so that he would read it, ponder on it, and prepare his apologies. This would make the term of confinement in his room worthwhile. At that time, I had no vision left and I didn't have a computer either. I grabbed a note pad and a pen. I began to furiously put my thoughts on paper. I had to make sure that my hand moved down after each line so as not to write over the same line. "Take this to your brother," I ordered one of his brothers as I handed him the two-page folded note.

A few moments later, he came back, gave me the note right back and said with a matter-of-fact tone, "He can't read this."

"What do you mean, he can't read this!" I responded with impatience.

"It's blank," was his nonchalant answer.

I had grabbed a pen with no ink!

Writing my story and sharing it with you has revealed many aspects of my life, ones that perhaps I would have overlooked. I can see clearly how close I came to living a life similar to that note for my son. Without Jesus to give me purpose and meaning, my life would have been blank...no message to give...no story to tell...no abundance to share!

I feel grateful because Jesus is not only my Lord and Savior but also my teacher—the greatest teacher of all. Using the eyes of my heart, He has taught me to see and follow the path that took me to the other side of adversity and affliction. "Though He give you the bread of adversity and the water of affliction, yet He will be with you to teach you—with your own eyes you will see your teacher" (Isaiah 30:20 TLB).

33

Last Step

S ince I love challenges, when someone says that I can't do something, I stop, think for a minute, and then turn to Jesus. He responds, giving me a spiritual wink as He whispers to my heart, "We can do it." Ever since I made him the Lord of my life, we have worked as a team in crucially important areas of my life and even in insignificant ones.

When my schedule became too full, I was forced to cut back some activities. The one at the bottom of the list and the first to go was the time I took to get a manicure. A friend convinced me to get acrylic nails, what a pain, why did I accept, because, you never outgrow peer pressure. It didn't take long for me to figure out this was not a good idea. An hour every two weeks for a "fill," while forced to listen to offensive talk shows blaring through the TV set throughout the salon! Sitting there with my hands behind that little curtain, why the curtain? I wasn't going to watch what they did anyway! I became annoyed because of the time I wasted— both my time and that of the person who had to take me there and bring me back from this little vanity trip.

My solution was to contact my Mary Kay beauty consultant. She would be able to provide me with all I needed to have the manicure done by whom? You guessed it...moi!! While I listened to my favorite teaching tapes or while my ears were occupied taking in other worthwhile material, I went to work. I followed the steps carefully, remove the old polish, and file them to shape, and base coat, next the color and finally the topcoat. Voila! My nails were done.

However, I thought I would have to administer CPR to my poor mother when she walked in the first time after I had achieved this task. With a shrill of horror she cried out, "What have you done to your hands!" I imagine that the bright color of the 'cherries jubilee' all around my fingernails were a sight to see! But...but what she hadn't seen was the last step. I had planned to soak my hands in warm soapy water in order to peel any polish residue that covered the areas around the fingernails. This last step is very, very important because then they are left with a look as if they were done in a salon. Yes, I most definitely get compliments on the shape and the way my fingernails look. Anyone need a manicure? I'm a pro now!

The last step in any worthwhile project is the key to its success. It is the step that brings it to a point where it can make sense. It is what allows it to come to a true completion.

Not long ago, I was asked to speak to a large group of women at an annual event. The comments I heard afterwards were very kind. They explained that I made them cry and I made them laugh. But my last step, my most important step, is always to point them to Jesus, and bring home a message filled with hope and encouragement.

The same applies in my work as an interpreter. As I close the call, my last step is also a most important one. With sincerity and a smile in my voice, I proceed to tell the client that it was a pleasure to help them. This expression of appreciation is the step that is necessary to leave them with a lasting positive impression.

People are creatures of habit, they say. I think that is true because that certainly describes Gene and me. We seem to follow the same bedtime routine night after night. While we're getting ready for bed and in between the buzzing of our electric toothbrushes, we exchange comments about our day. Then we proceed to take our last step. We both kneel down for prayer. Why kneel? Because Jesus said, "Again, I say to you that if two of you agree on earth concerning anything that they ask, it will be done for them by My Father in Heaven. For where two or three are gathered together in my name, I am there in the midst of them" (Matthew 18:19-20 NKJV).

Humbled before the presence of God, we ask for forgiveness. We thank Him for all the undeserved blessings and proceed to make our requests before God. These include praying for every aspect of our sons' lives, praying for our parents, friends, and those who ask us to pray for them. And, although praying together is possibly the most important part of our relationship, it is the last step before ending our day.

How well do you know your facts? See if you know the answer to this question. What is one of the major differences between Christianity and the other religions of the world? If you answered the last step, you're right! That last step, the most important step—the one that makes all the difference in the world!

Jesus was born and He died...but the last step is that He rose from the dead. He has risen and is alive! Not only alive but also actively impacting the lives of those who open their hearts to Him.

Do you find the resurrection hard to believe? Sounds too farfetched to you? You're not alone. A man named Josh McDowell thought the very same thing. He set out to prove that this was nothing but a fairy tale made up by weak men. You won't believe the facts and events he found out! I invite you to read two of his books: *Beyond Belief to Convictions* and *More than a Carpenter*.

Although my book is drawing to a close, I know God has not written the last chapter of my life. The last step is taken when I finally face Him in the glory of heaven. This is when I take up residence in the mansion He has prepared for me!

34

"How Can I Keep From Singing"

I shared with you at the beginning that I don't have any theological credentials. It's just me, my computer, my patient husband, and the support of some close friends. But with Jesus leading the project, there was no stopping me! But I have to be honest with you; I began this project with a certain amount of apprehension. I shared this with Gene and I asked him, "Do you really think someone would be interested in what I have to say? I have no experience in writing." His answer was what God needed me to hear. It was given in five simple words, "Honey, you have the Lord."

So I went ahead. My fingers began to dance on my trusty keyboard. I put my story in this book format so that you would be able to see just who Jesus is, what He is to me, and what He could be for you. You guessed it; I have a story to illustrate this.

You might think by now that I'm a vain person who still worries about wearing the right kind of make-up, even takes time to do her own manicure, and works hard at staying physically fit. If you thought that...hate to admit it, but you're right!

If that wasn't enough, I do go once in a great while to have a pedicure. Before you say, see, I knew she had a frivolous side to her, listen to this story first. My trips to get my pedicure became a blessed event for me. You read that right...a blessed event!

My mom took me to my appointment. As we stepped into the salon, the unmistakable strong scent of nail polish and other chemicals commonly used filled the air. As we walked past the waiting area, I could hear the sounds coming from the television, mixed with small talk between the nail techs and their customers. In the background, I heard the sound of a catchy tune coming from someone's cell phone.

The person at the desk informed me that the lady who was going to take care of me was no longer available. I was assigned to a young man named Bo. "What? I don't really want a guy to fool with my feet," I thought with annoyance. But I regained composure and reasoned, "Get a life. He's only going to slop some nail polish on your toe nails...get a grip on yourself!"

"Hi, Bo," I said confidently.

"Hi. This way," he replied.

My mom and I followed him. Once we agreed on a time she would pick me up, she left. I proceeded to sit on the chair next to the tub, which had another chair behind it. I patiently waited for him to begin his work on my feet. Once he came back, he said something that I just couldn't understand. I asked him to repeat what he said, but I still couldn't understand. It was later that I learned that he was new and had just arrived from Cambodia. Consequently, he knew very little English. This should be interesting, I thought.

Silence...I didn't know if he was in front of me or if he had walked away. Finally, I decided to give him a heads-up. "I'm blind, so I may need some..." I tried to inform him.

"Oh, blind... yes, hi!"

"No, my name is not blind, my name is Jan." I thought I should clarify.

About that time, he turned on the water machine. I really don't know what it does, but I do know that it makes a lot of steady noise. This sound normally would be no problem, but now every word he said to me was not only difficult to hear but almost impossible to understand. Nevertheless, we had a nice chat. What did we talk about? I have no clue! He would say something, and I would reply. Neither one of us could really understand one another. But it didn't matter because since I like to talk so much, there is little that gets in the way.

I have a sweet friend, Janet who says that I have "holy boldness." I guess she is right, because when it comes to sharing the goodness of the Lord with anyone, I don't have a shy bone in my body. This time, Bo opened the door to begin my usual way to bring Jesus into the conversation. When he finally turned the noisy water machine off, he commented, "You can't see? Why you hoppy?"

"Why am I happy when I'm blind?" I wanted to make sure I heard him right.

"Yes!" he responded.

I told him about Jesus. I told him that He was my friend and my Lord and I have Him in my life and in my heart. He made no comments one way or the other. Silence followed. Then he asked, "Who is Jesus?"

"What did you say?" I asked not believing my ears. I couldn't imagine anyone not having heard about Jesus. I had met people who would very boldly tell me that they don't believe in Him. Others who said that they believe in God and that they wish to know nothing else. But this was a first for me. I didn't know how to proceed. So, I asked him if he wanted to know about Jesus so that he could also be happy as I was.

"Hmmm...don know..." he chuckled.

Yes, we live in a politically correct society and we must be careful not to "offend" anyone or impose on them by bringing up the name of Jesus. But if neither the language barrier, nor the noisy machine could stop me, I wasn't going to let the shallow view of the world stop me either.

I told Bo that I would bring him a book called the Bible. I informed him that this book will tell him all about Jesus. I even told him that I would find one in Cambodian. It might take a while to find, but I was determined. I walked in for my next appointment with a Cambodian Bible in my arms. I handed it to him, telling him that it was a gift from me.

I knew that he might not know just what to do with this wonderful book. So I decided to include a letter for him. I wanted to choose words that were plain, basic, and easy to understand. I didn't want his limited English to get in the way. The letter said something like this:

Hi, Bo:

I got this Bible for you so that you can read about God. He is the father of Jesus. There are many stories for us to read in this wonderful book. But it is very important to know that these are not just stories, but events that really happened. They are all true.

When you read this Bible in your language, you will read all about Jesus, how He was born and where He was born. But, Bo, what is more important is to know why He came to this world. He came to pay for our sins (sins are things that we do which don't make God happy). Jesus didn't pay for our sins with money like I pay for my pedicure, but He paid with His life. How? On a cross. That was the way they punished bad people at that time. They thought he was a bad person.

Jesus said that if you believe in Him and ask Him into your heart like I did, He would let you come into heaven. That is a place that He made for all of us, but if you don't want Him in your life, there is another place where you would be separated from Him forever. Bo, this is a place you don't want to be!

I hope you will want to know more about Jesus and make Him your very best friend, too!

Thank you for letting me tell you about my God who makes me happy.

Jan

I had been exactly where Bo was, in the midst of a foreign culture, unable to speak the language, and feeling lost. His timid and insecure demeanor touched my heart. I so wanted to share with him the greatest gift I had—a life of confidence found in Christ. I guess I thought that in this case with Bo and me, the roles were reversed. He could see...but was spiritually blind.

You're probably asking yourself, what gives me the right to hold that opinion of someone? Actually, I agree with you. I do not have the right to judge anyone. Only God has that privilege. What I do have, however, is simply the confidence obtained from God's Word, "And are confident that you yourself are a guide to the blind, a light to those who are in darkness" (Romans 2:19 NKJV).

"How can I keep from singing," echo the lyrics of an old Christian song. I think that I wrote this book for the same reason. How can I keep from sharing what God has done in my life? How can I keep silent and not tell others of the treasure I found? Actually, my intent was not "to tell," but to demonstrate how God's power, love, and grace can take one beyond adversity. Not only for those like my friend Bo, but also those who might be faced with overwhelming pain or sorrow. I'd like to share with you what my prayer might be:

If I speak my convictions, sharing your truth and your love by using simple words as a tool...

They would just trickle down and fall like raindrops down a slippery rock. They would laugh with scorn and call me a fool!

But if my life should reflect your tender compassion, the power of your love that pierced through my pain...

Then they too shall call you their Savior, for their hearts will see clearly that a trust placed in you is never in vain.

They'll know for themselves that you're able, truly able, to conquer the darkness brought on by a sorrow...

You alone are the hope, the hope that dispels the doubts of tomorrow.

35

Good as Gold

"**D**o you know what these are?" asked my father as my brother and I saw with amazement the three somewhat large nuggets of gold. We were both too young to be able to appreciate the real value of these small treasures, nor the effort he went through to find them in an abandoned mine in Bolivia.

The year 1952 marked the end of one of the most destructive revolutions in Bolivia. As would be expected, one of the devastating results was the scarcity of work. Consequently, my father had to be creative in providing for the family. Once he had exhausted all possibilities, he decided to set out to look for gold...in the real sense. Bolivia had large natural resources of gold and silver. Unfortunately the sophisticated equipment used by businesses had previously cleaned out the gold from the mines and surrounding areas. However, after sifting the soil of random spots, he managed to find a few nuggets of gold. He brought them back home and for a long time after, this venture became the topic of conversation for the whole family. I remember the amazement with which I heard that story related to my brother and me. But what I was most impressed with was how this simple gold nugget turned into a beautiful ring for my mom.

In order to make the ring, there was a specific process that needed to take place. The first step was to purify the nugget. This was achieved by using acids to remove alloys or other impurities. It was then mixed with certain materials in order to make it a stronger substance because pure gold is soft and easy to bend. It was then ready to be subjected to the intense heat of a torch, melting it in order to place it in a mold. I remember admiring the intricately designed gold ring. But what was more fascinating to me was that it had started out as a simple shapeless gold nugget.

The Old Testament is replete with mentions of gold. Gold is referred to in a variety of ways. Sometimes as a sign of strength, wealth, honor, as well as forms of beauty. The man named Job knew about gold and its significance. He was probably familiar with the process that gold needed to undergo. He faced suffering and hardship difficult to imagine by anyone. His steady faith, unwavering trust in God, and his conviction to still persevere made him the example for all to follow. Referring to God, Job said, "But He knows the way that I take; when He has tested me, I shall come forth as gold" (Job 23:10 NKJV).

What I faced in my life doesn't compare to Job's suffering, but I would like to strive to emulate his faith and conviction.

I feel as though my life has followed the process of refinement in much the same way as gold. Jesus Christ has been the shield and protection that prevented the heat of suffering to melt me into despair. As a result, the adversity woven throughout my life has served to refine my heart. As the impurities are removed, there is room to hold the abundance, richness, and everlasting hope for a renewed life.

36

Developing a Portfolio for Life

"Have you not known? Have you not heard? The everlasting God, the LORD, the Creator of the ends of the earth, neither faints nor is weary. His understanding is unsearchable. He gives power to the weak, and to those who have no might He increases strength" (Isaiah 40:28-29 NKJV).

If I had been spared from the events that took place in my life, I could not have held the same conviction as I gave the answers to the questions in this passage. Each step of my journey brought to light the reply I would give without doubt or hesitation. Yes, not only have I heard, but I also have come to know this firsthand. The greatness of a loving God, who is the creator of all, renewed my strength, turned obstacles into opportunities, and transformed adversity into a renewed awareness of his abundance. He did for me just what he said He would do, "I have come that they might have life, and that they may have it more abundantly" (John 10:10 NKJV). Through Christ, this abundance became a reality for me at moments of emotional bankruptcy and when I lacked any other resources.

I try very hard to pay close attention when Gene shares any ideas, or comments about his job, our family, or any subject at all. To me, everything he says is important; but there is one topic that seems to lose my attention. It's the topic of finances. I have little interest in the ups and downs of our stock accounts, our 401K plans or bank accounts. I think that it's often a boring topic.

When it comes to putting together a diversified portfolio, however, I don't go to a financial adviser. I go to Jesus, my faithful adviser. Using the guide given in the Bible, I have developed my own portfolio...a spiritual one. This is where I draw my strength. I tap into its wealth, which includes the gold of his forgiveness, mercy, and His sustaining power. It contains the silver of His endless love, compassion, peace, and faithfulness. I bought stock in His promises that never lose their value and the returns are constant and abundant.

37

Set Free

I'd like to relate to you a conversation between a baby camel and his mother. He asked her, "Why do we have such large hoofs on our feet?"

Her answer was, "God made us that way for a very special reason," and she began her explanation. "The big hoofs are to keep us from sinking into the sand."

"Oh!" continued the baby camel, "and why the long eyelashes?"

"To protect our eyes from the sand," explained the mother.

"Why the big humps?"

"That is to store fat and have enough energy to go long distances in the hot desert!" was her answer.

"I see!" exclaimed the baby camel. "The big hoofs are to keep from sinking into the sand, the long eyelashes are to keep the sand from our eyes, and the humps are to store energy to travel long distances...then what are we doing in this cage in the middle of a zoo?"

Sometimes sin, addictions, or adversity may take away the freedom to enjoy the gifts God has given us. Much like these camels, we find ourselves stuck in a place where we are unable to live our lives fully, the way God intended us to live. Did you ever experience this? Perhaps you also find yourself "out of place" and confined behind the bars of pain due to any number of circumstances—a physical impairment, a painful divorce, financial struggles, cancer, loneliness, that constant search for someone or something, or even the death of a loved one. They can all create an emotional and spiritual cage, forming a prison of restrictive hopelessness.

If so, I have good news for you; Jesus has already removed these bars of confinement and is just waiting for you to walk out into freedom. I speak from experience when I tell you this; the most important thing to remember is that although the circumstances may remain the same, through Jesus, the freedom to live an abundant life is still available. Not the freedom from adversity but freedom from the bondage of its effects. In my case, my physical sight was not restored, nor did my son Joe come back to life, but Jesus set me free from the devastating aftermath of these events. He remains by my side, close enough to hear my every sigh, near enough to read my heart and hear every beat. He is so intimately close to me that He knows my every thought. But the best news of all is that He longs to do the same for you.

Something similar happened to David. He is probably one of my favorite people in the Bible. God blessed him in more ways than most, but eventually he still chose to succumb to temptation. He created for himself a cage of sin. But when he recognized his ways, he genuinely repented, turned to God, and experienced His merciful forgiveness. This reconnection with God brought to him the confidence, assurance, and protection he needed at times of desperation as his life was being threatened.

I invite you to follow the same steps David followed. He didn't look around at his circumstances; he looked up. There he found the answer. When you do the same, I am convinced that your heart will also echo with David's words, and you can say with conviction in your voice and confidence in your heart: "The LORD is my light and my salvation; Whom shall I fear? The LORD is the strength of my life; Of whom shall I be afraid?" (Psalm 27:1 NKJV).

A Final Note to the Reader

I want to thank you…thank you because if you got to the point at which you're reading this note, it means that you've given me the gift of your time as you read my story. In reading the pages of this book, you saw me walk down the aisle of life accompanied by great adversity. But I want you to know that you have given me the opportunity to leave that company behind. You have given me the joy of sharing the triumph I experienced through Christ. My prayer is that the episode of my blindness has pointed you to the light of His Word. And through the death of my child, I have pointed you to a life that can be full of unequaled hope, joy, and peace.

The wealth and richness God provided me with is much more than what I could use in a lifetime. For this reason, I related my story to you with a heart of gratitude and with the hope of sharing this wealth with you. If you care to accept it, I'm convinced that you too will see how Jesus will turn the trials you face today to treasures you will cherish tomorrow.

You're not just a reader and I'm not just a writer…you and I are friends now! Please keep in touch with me:

www.janeckles.com

PART III

STUDY GROUP GUIDE

I wonder if you were ever asked the question, "Do you believe in God?" I have, and my answer was always an emphatic, "Yes!" So what was the problem? Well, with me, it was that I believed **in God**, but I had to search my heart to find out if I **believed God** —did I believe in what He said.

This more direct question prompted me to develop this portion of the book. It is aimed to those who might want to consider the input given by God. The question is not if you believe in God, but do you believe what God says through His Word.

All of us have a variety of resources from which we draw our opinions, beliefs, values, and convictions. They vary from the religious teachings and doctrines we learned on our own, bits of information we gathered through our lifetime, beliefs taught to us by our parents. This study will focus on a greater source —the Word of God found in the Bible.

The discussion and thought-provoking questions are divided in sections to facilitate a certain number of sessions. Whether readers are participating in Bible studies or book club gatherings, the questions may be chosen and divided according to the discretion of the discussion leader.

SECTION 1

SEARCH YOUR HEART

New Kid on the Block

Jan moved to the U.S. from Bolivia. Being a foreigner meant that she felt out of place, inadequate, and conspicuously different from everyone else.

Perhaps you happen to be the "new kid" in this group. If that's the case, your heart certainly holds feelings of apprehension, hesitation about the dynamics of this group, or how well you will fit in.

As adults, are there still feelings of inadequacy in our lives? Share some areas in which you think we get caught trying to "fit in," be accepted, or be liked by those with whom we interact. How did your desire to "fit in" change or improve through the years?

God says:

For we dare not make ourselves of the number, or compare ourselves with some that commend themselves: but
they measuring themselves by themselves, and comparing
themselves among themselves, are not wise.

2 Corinthians 10:12

Adjustments

Jan had no choice but to adjust to a new culture, a new
language, and a new way of life. She struggled but was able
to do so. It wasn't difficult because she went through this
adjustment period as a child.

In reality, all of us have to learn to adjust to situations,
which may not be within our control. What emotions rule
your thinking when it comes to going into a new situation
that requires adjustment?

Do you resist changes because of a certain fear of read-
justing? How do you face changes? Do you "roll with the
punches," or are you affected emotionally by unplanned
changes?

God reassures:

Jesus Christ is the same yesterday, today, and forever.
Heb 13:8

Acceptance

Jan had no choice but accept her new life in a new world.
She suffered adjustment pains in difficult situations. As life
goes on, there are some things or situations, which we must
accept. Often they are not of our liking, or approval, but
acceptance is necessary.

Share a situation that you found yourself reluctantly accepting. Did you come to terms with it or is it still causing turmoil in your heart? Do you find it easier or more difficult to accept changes as you grow older?

God reassures:

And He said to me, "My grace is sufficient for you, for My strength is made perfect in weakness. Therefore most gladly I will rather boast in my infirmities, that the power of Christ may rest upon me."
II Corinthians 12:9

Humiliation

Jan experienced situations in which she felt humiliated and embarrassed. As a result, she was unable to let go, which created unnecessary insecurities as she grew up.

What has been your most embarrassing moment? Has that experience left any lingering emotional effect on you? (To be answered in your heart and not out loud.) If there is one thing you need to share with someone, one that would be very embarrassing, what would that be?

God says:

It is better to trust in the LORD
than to put confidence in man.
Psalm 118:8

So we may boldly say:

"The LORD is my helper;
I will not fear.
What can man do to me?"

Heb 13:6

For the LORD will be your confidence,
And will keep your foot from being caught
Prov 3:26

Self-Forgiveness

Jan had to learn to let go any guilty feelings about the life she lived apart from Jesus. She knew the forgiveness found in Him and moved on to enjoy His grace.

Are there any areas in your life where you find difficulty forgiving yourself? What do you understand about the forgiveness promised by God? Which is more difficult to do—forgive yourself or forgive someone else? Why?

God's promise:

For as the heavens are high above the earth,
So great is His mercy toward those who fear Him;
As far as the east is from the west,
So far has He removed our transgressions from us.
Psalm 103:11-12

If we confess our sins, He is faithful and just to forgive us our sins and to cleanse us from all unrighteousness.
I John 1:9

There is therefore now no condemnation to those who are in Christ Jesus, who do not walk according to the flesh, but according to the Spirit.
Rom 8:1

Values

Jan's life was sprinkled with values, which she drew from her family, and her native culture as well as the culture of her new home—the U.S. She longed to have financial success, fulfillment, and enjoyment of life. She held these values as a priority.

Those were her goals. What are yours? If being happy is your goal, what is happiness? Is happiness a realistic goal?

When it comes to values, where have you obtained your values from, your parents, peers, your own research, or your experiences?

God instructs:

I beseech you therefore, brethren, by the mercies of God, that you present your bodies a living sacrifice, holy, acceptable to God, which is your reasonable service. And do not be conformed to this world, but be transformed by the renewing of your mind, that you may prove what is that good and acceptable and perfect will of God. Rom 12:1-2

He has shown you, O man, what is good;
And what does the LORD require of you
But to do justly,
To love mercy,
And to walk humbly with your God?
Micah 6:8

Choices

Jan had to choose her dating companions. She used a certain criteria in order to pick the right one for her.

What criteria did you use to choose your partner? If single, what criteria do you have in mind for your partner for life? Looking back when you chose your partner, would you do it differently if you had to do it over again? Besides your husband, whom would you choose as your most intimate spiritual partner? Why?

God warns:

How can a young man cleanse his way? By taking heed according to Your word.
Psalm 119:9

The steps of a good man are ordered by the LORD,
And He delights in his way.
Though he fall, he shall not be utterly cast down;
For the LORD upholds him with His hand.
Psalm 37:23-24

Coping

When Jan and Gene faced the initial blow of her losing her sight, they first looked to their own inner resources for comfort and guidance.

When faced with adversity, where do you turn to first? When looking for answers, what criteria do you use in order to determine the reliability of the answer?

Share a situation when you've found yourself unable to cope. What did you do? How do you know if you're coping with adversity in a healthy manner?

God offers:

Cast your burdens on the Lord, and he shall sustain you"
Psalm 55:22

The Lord is good, a stronghold in the day of trouble; and

he knows those who trust in him.
Nahum 1:7

Disappointments

Jan found disappointment when she looked to for-tunetellers, new-age healers, horoscopes, psychics, and the like for answers.

Where have you turned for help and guidance. Did you find valuable information, direction and reassurance from any of them? Have you been disappointed by any of them? Was the monetary price worth the results?

God warns:

I will instruct you and teach you in the way you should go;
I will guide you with My eye.
Psalm 32:8

Show me Your ways, O LORD;
Teach me Your paths.
Lead me in Your truth and teach me,
For You are the God of my salvation;
On You I wait all the day.
Psalm 25:4-5

Reassurance

When Jan hit rock bottom and her husband informed her that he found someone else to lean on and confide in, she was devastated.

Have you ever experienced a disappointment, which was too difficult to bear? (It's not necessary to share the details with the group.) What was your first reaction? Was it anger, self-pity, revenge, fear, or guilt?

Where did you find reassurance? How long did it take you to find the reassuring answer?

God commands:

For the mountains shall depart
And the hills be removed,
But My kindness shall not depart from you,
Nor shall My covenant of peace be removed,"
Says the LORD, who has mercy on you.
Isaiah 54:10
The LORD is near to all who call upon Him,
To all who call upon Him in truth.
Psalm 145:18

Someone to Turn to

When her world was falling apart, Jan learned that there was someone she could turn to in the midst of her pain. After trying to resolve the situation on her own, she turned it over to Jesus. When suffering a painful event, did you find someone to whom you could just "turn it all over to?" Was there someone who was able to guarantee you a solution? If so, who was it? Was there a place where you turn to and found a trustworthy answer? If yes, where?

God offers:

Be of good courage, and he shall strengthen your heart, all ye that hope in the LORD.
Psalms 31:24

Casting all your care upon Him, for He cares for you
I Peter 5:7

For I know the thoughts that I think toward you, says the LORD, thoughts of peace and not of evil, to give you a future and a hope.
Jeremiah 29:11

The LORD is my rock and my fortress and my deliverer;
My God, my strength, in whom I will trust;
My shield and the horn of my salvation, my stronghold.
Psalm 18:2

Unexpected Results

Jan found that God exceeded her expectations when she prayed. This took place when she chose to open her heart to God's Word.

In moments of painful struggle, did you ever find anyone who provided you with better-than-expected answers? What dictates your path as you look for answers? Is it your judgment, your resources, your knowledge, or your intuition?

Share some instances where you found that God was the last person you turned to for help.

God offers:

And if we know that He hears us, whatever we ask, we know that we have the petitions that we have asked of Him.
I John 5:15

"It shall come to pass
That before they call, I will answer;
And while they are still speaking, I will hear."
Isaiah 65:24

I am the vine, you are the branches. He who abides in Me, and I in him, bears much fruit; for without Me you

can do nothing.
John 15:5

Understanding the Word

Jan's initial attitude toward the Bible and the individual verses was one of arrogance and judgment.

Have you ever attempted to read the Bible and found it didn't make sense? What prompted you to open the Bible? What were your feelings about reading the Bible? Have you ever challenged what the Bible said?

Who influenced you the most regarding the meaning of the Bible and its impact? What were your thoughts as you read the way Jan applied God's Word in each specific situation?

God instructs:

All Scripture is given by inspiration of God, and is profitable for doctrine, for reproof, for correction, for instruction in righteousness, that the man of God may be complete, thoroughly equipped for every good work.
II Tim 3:16-17

Forgiveness

Jan was guided by Jesus' example to forgive. She forgave her husband. As a result, she found peace and renewed hope for her marriage. Jan did not "forget" what Gene had done, but she chose to look at his actions through Christ's eyes—with forgiveness and compassion.

What is the most difficult obstacle you found in trying to forgive someone? Do you believe in "forgive and forget?" What effect does it have on you when you fail to forgive? Have you ever attempted to seek revenge against someone?

What were the results?

God commands:

And be kind to one another, tenderhearted, forgiving one another, just as God in Christ forgave you.
Ephesians 4:32

bearing with one another, and forgiving one another, if anyone has a complaint against another; even as Christ forgave you, so you also must do.
Colossians 3:13

"For if you forgive men their trespasses, your heavenly Father will also forgive you."
Matt 6:14

But love your enemies, do good, and lend, hoping for nothing in return; and your reward will be great, and you will be sons of the Most High. For He is kind to the unthankful and evil. Therefore be merciful, just as your Father also is merciful
"Judge not, and you shall not be judged. Condemn not, and you shall not be condemned. Forgive, and you will be forgiven. Give, and it will be given to you: good measure, pressed down, shaken together, and running over will be put into your bosom. For with the same measure that you use, it will be measured back to you."
Luke 6:35-38

Determination

Jan found confidence in Jesus, and she was determined that she would no longer take control. She let God take control of her life. The results were better than she hoped for.

What circumstances have you felt you need to be in control of? Have you tried to take charge of your weight, your children, your job, your husband, a friend?

What do you find controls you? When do you find the greatest need to be freed from what seems to bind or control you?

God offers:

Stand fast therefore in the liberty by which Christ has made us free, and do not be entangled again with a yoke of bondage.
Galatians 5:1

Whoever has no rule over his own spirit, is like a city broken down, without walls
Prov 25:28

A fool vents all his feelings, but a wise man holds them back.
Prov 29:11

Therefore gird up the loins of your mind, be sober, and rest your hope fully upon the grace that is to be brought to you at the revelation of Jesus Christ;
I Peter 1:13

Surrender

Jan was forced to surrender her situation. The load she carried—her blindness, her marriage, the future of her children, her life—was tremendous. As she surrendered all of this, she found freedom, peace, and the ability to enjoy life once again.

Are there any areas of your life that need surrendering?

What keeps you from releasing them to God? Have you tried to do this and found that it was more difficult than you thought? Why?

God's instruction:

Therefore submit to God. Resist the devil and he will flee from you.
James 4:7

Unity

Jan's marriage survived many trials. She and Gene learned the importance of prayer. It was uncomfortable at first but once establishing a prayer base, they found that God honored them beyond their expectations.

What do you find is the greatest obstacle preventing you from praying together with your husband? What type of prayers are you accustomed to? What interferes with your prayer time on a regular basis?

Share a situation where a prayer was answered but in a different way than expected.

God reassures us:

Now this is the confidence that we have in Him, that if we ask anything according to His will, He hears us. And if we know that He hears us, whatever we ask, we know that we have the petitions that we have asked of Him.
I John 5:14-15

Therefore I say to you, whatever things you ask when you pray, believe that you receive them, and you will have them.
Mark 11:24

Again I say to you that if two of you agree on earth concerning anything that they ask, it will be done for them by My Father in heaven. For where two or three are gathered together in My name, I am there in the midst of them."

Matt 18:19-20

SECTION 2

PARENTING

Priorities

J an's focus was not in the education, professional success, or sports achievements for her sons. She focused on the spiritual development of her children.

What is your opinion of those who claim that it's not wise to "cram religion down the throats" of your children? Would you agree with the opinion that children need to grow up and choose their faith? Why? What are the dangers of not providing the solid, trustworthy truth to our children?

How would you react if your child indicated that he/she was going to join a cult? Where do you go to find direction and guidance in your parenting efforts?

God's input:

Train up a child in the way he should go,

And when he is old he will not depart from it
Prov 22:6

And you, fathers, do not provoke your children to wrath,
but bring them up in the training and admonition of the Lord.
Ephesians 6:4

If thy children will keep my covenant and my testimony that I shall teach them, their children shall also sit
upon thy throne for evermore.
Psalms 132:12

Protection

Jan believed in her son's spiritual protection more than
in their physical protection.

What area of protection is most important for you
regarding your children? What is the best way to protect
them? Is there a specific fear you have in your heart about
your children?

Comparing to the way you were raised, what would you
do differently for your children?

God reassures:

Because you have made the LORD, who is my refuge,
Even the Most High, your dwelling place,
No evil shall befall you,
Nor shall any plague come near your dwelling;
For He shall give His angels charge over you,
To keep you in all your ways.
Psalm 91:9-11

And do not fear those who kill the body but cannot kill
the soul. But rather fear Him who is able to destroy both

soul and body in hell.
Matt 10:28

The Battle

Jan found that the world had a strong pull for her sons.
She battled this influence with prayer and Biblical teachings.

What is the greatest influence for your children outside
the home? How do you prepare your children to face the
temptations? If it were up to you, what values would be the
most important for your children?

What are your feelings regarding the partner your child
chooses for life? What advice would give him/her in choosing a spouse?

What is the best example you can give your child? Why?
Will it also be a priority for them?

God's Word:

"Do not lay up for yourselves treasures on earth, where
moth and rust destroy and where thieves break in and steal;"
Matt 6:19

But seek first the kingdom of God and His righteousness, and all these things shall be added to you.
Matt 6:33

SECTION 3

FACING ADVERSITY

Trials in Life

Jan's life was touched by enormous adversity, some of which could have caused despair and devastation.

How would you have handled each situation if you were in her shoes?

- Her blindness
- The betrayal of her husband
- The financial stress
- The death of her son

If she didn't know Christ, where would you direct her for guidance? If the Bible weren't your first choice, what would be another option? What would you have done differently if you were in Jan's situation?

God's input:

In this you greatly rejoice, though now for a little while, if need be, you have been grieved by various trials, that the genuineness of your faith, being much more precious than gold that perishes, though it is tested by fire, may be found to praise, honor, and glory at the revelation of Jesus Christ,
I Peter 1:6-7

The LORD will guide you continually,
And satisfy your soul in drought,
And strengthen your bones;
You shall be like a watered garden,
And like a spring of water, whose waters do not fail
Isaiah 58:11

Your ears shall hear a word behind you, saying,
"This is the way, walk in it,"
Whenever you turn to the right hand
Or whenever you turn to the left.
Isaiah 30:21

Eternity

Jan's belief in God and His promise for eternity became a reality when her son's life ended on earth.

What are your feelings about eternity? What promise about eternity is the most reassuring for you? What were the teachings you received about eternity?

God's Word:

And this is the testimony: that God has given us eternal life, and this life is in His Son. He who has the Son has life; he who does not have the Son of God does not have life.

These things I have written to you who believe in the name of the Son of God, that you may know that you have eternal life, and that you may continue to believe in the name of the Son of God.

I John 5:11-13

For the wages of sin is death, but the gift of God is eternal life in Christ Jesus our Lord.

Rom 6:23

And I give them eternal life, and they shall never perish; neither shall anyone snatch them out of My hand.

John 10:28

Brevity of Life

Jan's renewed awareness of the brevity of life was emphasized after she lost her nineteen-year-old son.

What would you like to leave as a mark after you're gone from this earth? After believing in the promises of God, has your perception about death changed? Do you believe in heaven? Why? What is the most reassuring aspect about heaven for you?

God's Word:

Whereas you do not know what will happen tomorrow. For what is your life? It is even a vapor that appears for a little time and then vanishes away.

James 4:14

"Let not your heart be troubled; you believe in God, believe also in Me. In My Father's house are many mansions; if it were not so, I would have told you. I go to prepare a place for you. And if I go and prepare a place for you,

I will come again and receive you to Myself; that where I am, there you may be also.

John 14:1-3

But as it is written:

"Eye has not seen, nor ear heard,
Nor have entered into the heart of man
The things which God has prepared for those who love Him."

I Cor 2:9

For since the beginning of the world
Men have not heard nor perceived by the ear,
Nor has the eye seen any God besides You,
Who acts for the one who waits for Him
Isaiah 64:4

Hope

Jan never lost hope. Even when her son died, her hope was renewed because she relied on God's trustworthy promises.

What do you rely on for hope? What characteristic of Jesus brings the most hope to your heart? As a Christian, are there any circumstances, which would be considered, as hopeless? What advice would you give to someone who feels hopeless?

God's Word:

For I know the thoughts that I think toward you, says the LORD, thoughts of peace and not of evil, to give you a future and a hope.

Jeremiah 29:11

Behold, the eye of the LORD is on those who fear Him,
On those who hope in His mercy,
Psalm 33:18

But those who wait on the LORD
Shall renew their strength;
They shall mount up with wings like eagles,
They shall run and not be weary,
They shall walk and not faint.
Isaiah 40:31

Joy

Jan learned what "happiness" was not. She started out thinking that happiness meant financial security, health, and good relationships. She found, disappointment, in all three. At different points of her life she found that they could all be fleeting.

What is your definition of "happiness?" Have you found happiness in your life? What would you say is the difference between joy and happiness? Have you found something or someone who brings lasting joy to your life? Can you guarantee that person/thing will always be there?

God offers:

If you keep My commandments, you will abide in My love, just as I have kept My Father's commandments and abide in His love. These things I have spoken to you, that My joy may remain in you, and that your joy may be full.
John 15:10-11

Security

Jan's security initially was in her husband's income. When faced with financial collapse, they both turned to draw from their "spiritual" portfolio. This spiritual "account" proved to be more valuable and reliable than any financial resource.

What does "security" mean to you? What have you put your trust in? Is financial security your goal? Why? Why not?

What is the one thing you fear will take your "security" away? Have you thought about what would be the one "thing" or person without whom you couldn't live?

God commands:

Some trust in chariots, and some in horses;
But we will remember the name of the LORD our God.
Psalm 20:7
The LORD is my rock and my fortress and my deliverer;
My God, my strength, in whom I will trust;
My shield and the horn of my salvation, my stronghold
Psalm 18:2

God is our refuge and strength,
A very present help in trouble
Psalm 46:1

Love

Jan found love when she understood that Jesus was the one who loved her enough to die for her.

What does true love mean to you? What are your expectations from someone who affirms they love you? Did someone who claimed he/she loved you ever disappoint you? In what way?

Have you ever felt that you gave love but didn't get it in return? If so, what was the main emotion ruling your heart? What does "truly loving someone" mean to you?

God's meaning of love:

For God so loved the world that He gave His only begotten Son, that whoever believes in Him should not perish but have everlasting life.
John 3:16

Love suffers long and is kind; love does not envy; love does not parade itself, is not puffed up; does not behave rudely, does not seek its own, is not provoked, thinks no evil; does not rejoice in iniquity, but rejoices in the truth; bears all things, believes all things, hopes all things, endures all things. Love never fails. But whether there are prophecies, they will fail; whether there are tongues, they will cease; whether there is knowledge, it will vanish away.
I Cor 13:4-8

Peace

Jan's peace was viciously taken away when Joe died. However, the peace in her heart was restored through Jesus and His promises, which proved to be trustworthy.

What takes your peace away on a daily basis? Worry takes peace in the heart and replaces it with anxiety. What is your main source of worry? Why? What have you done in the past to regain that peace in your heart? Do you feel at peace right now? Why? Why not? When your life seems to be in turmoil—where do you look for lasting peace?

Was there ever a point in your life when you felt unloved? Why? What is the one most meaningful way in which another person can demonstrate their love for you?

Where do you seek to find lasting and true love?

God's love:

And the peace of God, which surpasses all understanding, will guard your hearts and minds through Christ Jesus.
Phil 4:7

You will keep him in perfect peace,
Whose mind is stayed on You,
Because he trusts in You.
Isaiah 26:3

For to be carnally minded is death, but to be spiritually minded is life and peace.
Rom 8:6

Therefore, having been justified by faith, we have peace with God through our Lord Jesus Christ,
Rom 5:1

Peace I leave with you, My peace I give to you; not as the world gives do I give to you. Let not your heart be troubled, neither let it be afraid.
John 14:27

CPSIA information can be obtained at www.ICGtesting.com
Printed in the USA
BVOW02s0626160415

396246BV00001B/109/P